Norfolk Landowners

since 1880

Pam Barnes

Centre of East Anglian Studies
University of East Anglia

1993

ISBN 0 906219 32 9

Published by the Centre of East Anglian Studies, University of East Anglia, Norwich. Printed by the Printing Unit, University of East Anglia, Norwich

A note on the cover illustration: Bylaugh Hall.

John Lombe acquired the 600 acre Bylaugh estate in 1796 from Richard Lloyd in settlement of a gambling debt. When he died in 1817 he left a considerable amount of money in a trust fund earmarked for building a hall upon the site. Eventually, between 1850 and 1852, the house was built, by order of the Court of Chancery - hence the inscription on the masonry above the principal entrance 'Ex Jussu Curiae Cancellariae'.

The house was designed by Charles Barry (son of Sir Charles who was the architect for the Houses of Parliament) and Richard Banks, and was built in limestone blocks from Kiveton Park near Sheffield, the same stone as in the Houses of Parliament. Large drags with four or even six horses conveyed large blocks of stone to Bylaugh from Dereham Station. One hundred and ninety workmen were employed in its construction, including Italians for the decorative plaster work and a team of German decorators. The Norwich Mercury in February 1851 was of the opinion that: 'Neither Holkham nor Houghton, those Norfolk wonders, can compare with it for either appearance or comfort'. In fact, Bylaugh was never a building of distinction, and Pevsner described it only as a 'conspicuous ruin'. But it was a romantic building, built more in the style of an Italian palazzo than a Norfolk country house. It had a magnificent salon with a series of pilasters with Corinthian capitals in the centre position. Six splendid reception rooms opened on to this salon which had a panel-carved roof and plaques finely modelled in white and gold auto relief. But still money remained in trust, so the clock tower, lodges and nine miles of wall were built before the fund was used.

The family remained at Bylaugh for sixty-five years, after which the estate was sold. There was no immediate buyer for the house, and the threat of demolition was averted with the timely purchase of Bylaugh Hall by the Marsh family of Warwick, who retained it until 1948. Once again its future was threatened when a licence to demolish was applied for, but this was refused by the Ministry of Works. The Ministry of Town and Country Planning advised that it would be placed on the Protected Buildings list, and in the meantime the Ministry of Works granted a licence to demolish!

Bylaugh was pulled down in 1950, exactly 100 years after work on the house had been started. Noel Spencer's painting portrays the ghostly facade which is all that remains of Bylaugh Hall.

Contents

Chapter Three

Chapter Four

Conclusion   83

Acknowledgements

I am indebted to the many Norfolk landowners who responded so readily to my requests for information. They were courteous, explicit and generous with their help. In view of the difficulties experienced by researchers on landownership elsewhere, this kindness confirms my impression that they 'do different' in Norfolk. Lord Walsingham spared time to tell me about Merton, and both Bryan Hall and Michael Sayer drew upon their seemingly limitless knowledge of Norfolk estates and landowners to supply me with helpful information.

I am grateful for the assistance of the staff at the Norfolk Records Office who sought out sales catalogues and many other papers for me. Miss Jean Kennedy, Archivist, went out of her way to list records of Norfolk landowners which might be useful in my research, and I appreciate her help and also that of the Local History librarians in Norwich, who advised and assisted me. The Nelson Atkins Museum in Kansas City, U.S.A. provided me with a reproduction of Benjamin West's marriage portrait of John Custance and his wife of Weston Longville, and generously allowed me to include it.

For patient guidance when it came to printing I thank Mavis Wesley of the Centre of East Anglian Studies at the University of East Anglia, and for help in assembling photographs my thanks are due to John Marshall of the Local Studies Library, and to C.J.C. Bailey, Neil Foster, Lady Harrod, Kit Martin, Ralph Cross and Anglia Lead Ltd, also to Clifford Middleton for reproducing these photographs. It was kind of Alan Mackley to allow me to include his line drawing of Haveringland Hall, and most generous of Mr and Mrs George Schroeder who presented me with Noel Spencer's painting of Bylaugh Hall to mark the publication of this book.

Without the help of my son, Stephen, I would never have laboured to convert my doctoral thesis into a book had he not persuaded me to abandon my ancient typewriter in favour of a computer. With commendable patience he instructed, reassured and then rescued me in the many ensuing crises.

But my prime debt is to Dr Richard Wilson of the University of East Anglia, who supervised my thesis and encouraged me to write this book. I value his keen criticism, guidance and wisdom and thank him most sincerely.

HORNING 1992   P.B.

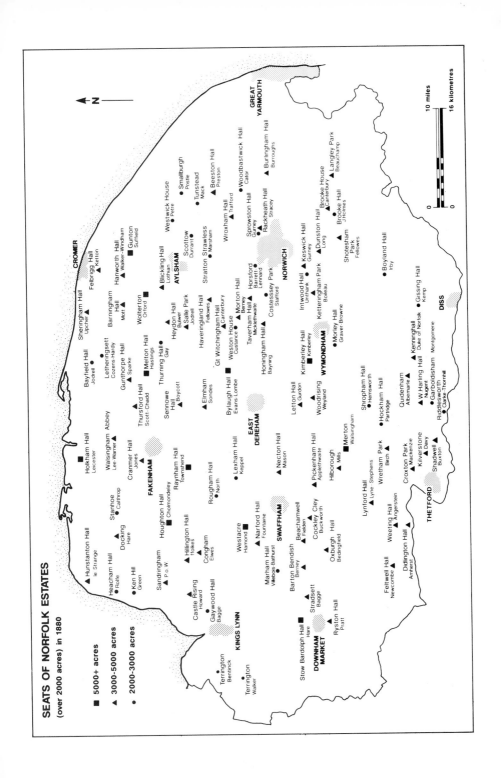

SEATS OF NORFOLK ESTATES
(over 2000 acres) in 1880

← N ⎯

Legend:
- ■ 5000+ acres
- ▲ 3000-5000 acres
- ● 2000-3000 acres

10 miles

16 kilometres

GREAT YARMOUTH

CROMER

NORWICH

DISS

AYLSHAM

WYMONDHAM

EAST DEREHAM

FAKENHAM

SWAFFHAM

THETFORD

KINGS LYNN

DOWNHAM MARKET

Woodbastwick Hall Cator
Burlingham Hall Burroughs
Beeston Hall Preston
Tunstead Mack
Smallburgh Postle
Westwick House Petre
Langley Park Beauchamp
Brooke House Canterbury
Brooke Hall J.Holmes
Shotesham Park Fellowes
Dunston Hall Long
Rackheath Hall Stracey
Sprowston Hall Gurney
Keswick Hall Gurney
Scottow Durrant
Stratton Strawless Marsham
Wroxham Hall Trafford
Felbrigg Hall Ketton
Sheringham Hall Upcher
Bayfield Hall Jodrell
Hanworth Hall Walker-Windham
Gunton Suffield
Blickling Hall Lothian
Barningham Hall Mott
Wolterton Orford
Letheringsett Cozens-Hardy
Gunthorpe Hall Sparke
Melton Hall Hastings
Heydon Hall Bulwer
Salle Park Jodrell
Haveringland Hall Fellowes
Morton Hall Canterbury
Weston House Custance
Taverham Hall Micklethwaite
Horsford Barrett
Horstead Lennard
Costesssey Park Stafford
Intwood Hall Unthank
Ketteringham Park Boileau
Boyland Hall Irby
Gissing Hall Kemp
Kenninghall Duke of Norfolk
W Harling Hall Nugent
Garboldisham Montgomerie
Riddlesworth Clarke-Thornhill
Quidenham Albemarle
Kimberley Hall Kimberley
Morley Hall Graver-Browne
Shropham Hall Hemsworth
Hockham Hall Partridge
Wretham Park Birch
Croxton Park Mackenzie
Kilverstone Davy
Shadwell Buxton
Thursford Hall Scott-Chadd
Sennowe Hall Boycott
Thurning Hall Gay
Elmham Sondes
Gt Witchingham Hall Berney
Honingham Hall Bayning
Letton Hall Gurdon
Woodrising Weyland
Bylaugh Hall Evans-Lombe
Lexham Hall Keppel
Necton Hall Mason
Pickenham Hall Applethwaite
Hilborough Mills
Merton Walsingham
Lynford Hall Lyne-Stephens
Weeting Hall Angerstein
Didlington Hall Amherst
Feltwell Hall Newcombe
Holkham Hall Leicester
Walsingham Abbey Lee-Warner
Cranmer Hall Jones
Raynham Hall Townshend
Houghton Hall Cholmondeley
Rougham Hall North
Hillington Hall Ffolkes
Sandringham P.o.W
Houghton Hall Cholmondeley
Stanhoe Calthrop
Docking Hare
Hunstanton Hall le Strange
Heacham Hall Rolfe
Ken Hill Green
Castle Rising Howard
Gaywood Hall Bagge
Terrington Bentinck
Terrington Walker
Stow Bardolph Hall Hare
Stradsett Bagge
Ryston Hall Pratt
Barton Bendish Berney
Beachamwell Fielden
Cockley Cley Buckworth
Oxburgh Hall Bedingfield
Marham Hall Villebois-Bathurst
Narford Hall Fountaine
Westacre Hamond
Congham Elwes

Introduction

Between 1781 and 1881 the number of people living in England and Wales rose from 7.5 million to 26 million. This burgeoning population could be sustained mainly from home-grown food supplies until the early decades of the nineteenth century by improvements in the efficiency of farming, but continuing population expansion outstripped the country's productive capacity and further growth depended upon food imports, bought in exchange for exports of coal and manufactured goods. Gradually, therefore, the economy became less dependent upon agriculture, and the power base shifted from the landowners to manufacturers and businessmen, the latter group also including those entrepreneurial landowners who became directly involved in the development of industry and commerce. The manifestations of this transfer of power eventually became apparent in the political arena. Whereas traditionally ancient wealth ruled and legislated, increasingly from the mid-nineteenth century the men of commerce and industry were elbowing their way forward and demanding their say in the government of a country which became largely dependent upon their initiative. Ruling families were edged aside, and by 1885 the landed class had lost its clear majority in the House of Commons, although its influence in the Lords was retained until 1910.

Most of the country's wealth was in the hands of the landowners. Their fortunes had been inherited, although there had always been an influx of newcomers keen to purchase estates with profits accumulated through industrial or commercial enterprise. But in the financial as well as the political sphere there was evidence of decline because income from the land dwindled in the late nineteenth century due to a massive depression in agriculture, which bore down heavily on agricultural landlords once rent levels had adjusted to the downturn. By the 1880s landowners were forced to accept stringent rent cuts, and substantial reduction of income, however abundant, created serious problems. The whole concept of landownership, not only as a way of life but also as a means of investment, was undermined when the meagre returns from landowning compared unfavourably with alternative forms of investment. The image of landed aristocrat or country squire lost some of its appeal. It is significant that the brewers, diamond millionaires and magnates of industry who clustered around King Edward Vll did not even aspire to ownership of large estates, and were often content to buy or even rent a country house in the home counties enclosed within a few hundred acres of parkland. A title was still an enviable acquisition at the turn of the century, but the newly rich were less easily enticed into agricultural commitment.

Queen Victoria's death marked the end of an era of landownership as an institution comprehensible to the Victorians. In this book I trace the elements of change which occurred in the pattern of landowning for the two subsequent generations of owners. It is not easy to convey the pathos of disruption and anxiety which underlay decisions to part with family heirlooms and to make final breaks with tradition. However, we can determine the solutions applied by the landowners to relieve their financial distress, and case histories from the 106 families who occupied Norfolk estates containing 2,000 or more acres will be used to illustrate reactions to the long downturn in agricultural prosperity. Norfolk is especially suitable for such a study, for it was, and still is, one of the prime cereal growing areas, vulnerable to the importation of foreign corn and therefore particularly subject to swings from prosperity to depression. When Norfolk farmers sneeze not only landowners but also a considerable cross-section of the community connected with trade, commerce and the professions in the county catches a cold, for agriculture is still the linchpin of the Norfolk economy. On the other hand, a thriving agricultural industry cushions the county against national economic downturns. In the early 1980s, for instance, Norfolk remained relatively immune to the industrial depression.

Surveying the history of landownership within one county produces a microcosmic picture which fills a gap in our knowledge. If similar research could be undertaken for, say, a dairying county in the South West and another in the vicinity of the northern manufacturing belt, then comparisons could be drawn which would make a useful contribution to historical perception. Public interest in the landowners has increased, partly as a result of the growing passion for visiting country houses, and there is a call for more information on their survival or reasons for decline. How far, one may ask, was the break-up of estates due to mismanagement and debt accumulation rather than to the depression and tax demands? Active land campaigners would have argued forcibly for the former, but this view was perhaps biased for land reform was one facet of the political power struggle of the new wealth creators.

Prices paid for estates have been ascertained from reliable sources, mainly the *Estates Gazette*, from estate papers in the Norfolk Records Office and newspaper reports (especially the *Eastern Daily Press*). The difficulty in citing these figures, as with rent levels, is that inflation distorts the figures so that a calculator is needed to relate nineteenth century prices to today's values. Suffice it to cite the *Economist*'s calculation that £1 in 1992 is worth six old pence (2.5p) in 1933 money[1].

The implications underlying this account of the tribulations of Norfolk landowners during the last, long agricultural depression are that history could repeat itself. Many landowners in the 1990s will be able to relate to the experiences of past generations. The agricultural cycle, of depression and recovery, boom and decline, affects us all, however remote our connections with farming. There is a close link between agricultural prosperity and the state of the economy generally: in the nineteenth century both prospered until a sharp decline in land values and income coincided with the Great Depression (1873-1896). The link was still apparent in the interwar years, and interrupted after 1945 only as a result of belated state support for agriculture. Since the 1980s the agricultural industry has increasingly been subject to market forces and the link is again discernible. If governments fail to support their farmers adequately, then existing qualms over the future of British agriculture will be justified.

[1]   *Economist* 8-14 August, 1992, p.11.

Chapter One
Depression in Agriculture

The impact of depression

The 1850s and 1860s had been the 'Golden Years' of agriculture. Prosperity was taken for granted on the assumption that the palmy days would continue indefinitely. Landowners drew up irrevocable wills and generous family settlements on the calculation that estate income would amply suffice to fulfil future obligations, and they often borrowed heavily on the security of their estates. But after 1875 a long period of depression wrecked estate finances, and family commitments became an impossible burden, while debts, so cheerfully negotiated in the years of prosperity, became impossible to service.

The agricultural depression coincided with a world economic recession in which prices of all raw materials were seriously undermined. At the same time there was an industrial depression in Britain which now faced competition from other newly-industrialising countries. Added to this, the difficulties of the agricultural industry were compounded because the strength and profitability of British farming were disastrously affected after the early 1870s by an ever-increasing supply of food imports entering the British market.

The seriousness of the depression was underestimated in its early stages. Initially the downturn was attributed to a series of atrocious summers in Britain throughout the years 1875-1879, which caused bad harvests and encouraged disease amongst farm stock. Even informed sources were deceived: Sir James Caird put weather first as a cause of depression in his evidence to the Duke of Richmond's Commission in 1881. Later the Duke of Bedford criticised this misjudgment:

Agriculturalists and the nation at large were alike insensible to the real character of the depression.... It is easy to be wise after the event, but it is strange that a catastrophe which was no longer merely impending but had actually taken place should have been regarded by those best able to judge as a passing cloud.[1]

Delay in acknowledging the full economic significance of the depression engendered optimistic anticipation of early improvement and resulted in short-term, *ad hoc* solutions. The first intimation to landowners of tenants' difficulties was delay in rent payment. Pleas for postponement were made, until the harvest was gathered in, or the livestock ready for market. On many estates rent arrears mounted, and at first were allowed to accrue, until it became apparent that the backlog of debt was becoming irredeemable. The landowner's response, quite rationally after only a couple of disappointing harvests, was to grant temporary allowances in the form of remissions and abatements until seasons improved. Generous remissions were often granted, in the region of thirty to fifty per cent of the annual rental, but they determinedly refused to allow more permanent rent reductions. They reasoned that rents could be adjusted with more flexibility through abatements than through formal reductions, and allowances could be varied selectively in favour of regular rent-payers and the more industrious tenants. But as far as tenants were concerned, abatements were unsatisfactory, for their temporary nature was held to be a hindrance to long-term planning, and abatements had the further disadvantage of not granting eligibility for re-assessment of rates which might have accompanied a more permanent rent reduction. Unfortunately for the tenants, the depression had lasted fifteen years before most landowners agreed to a permanent reduction of nominal rents.

Failure of landowners to understand the situation exacerbated the problems of farmers. The majority of farms at that time were tenanted, therefore the policy decisions of comparatively few landowners made a significant impact on farming initiative. Even in Norfolk, where there was a strong contingent of owner-occupiers, half a million acres out of a total agricultural area of 1,250,000 acres were contained in 106 estates comprising

2,000 or more acres, and there were many smaller estates. Eleven Norfolk families between them owned 175,000 acres.

Landowners were not as grasping nor as unconcerned for the welfare of tenants as the land reformers portrayed them. In fact, it was in the interest of both owner and farmer for tenants to remain solvent. It was the imperfect realisation of the true plight of tenant farmers which delayed appropriate financial assistance from landlords, and resulted in the ruin of good tenants. But from about 1885 the urgency of the situation made sufficient impact for landowners to grant significant reductions in contractual rents rather than allowing temporary abatements. On the 6,283 acre Blickling estate, for example, the nominal rental income from the thirty-eight farms fell from £7,185 in 1874 to £5,970 in 1888, and fell further in 1893 to £5,430.[2] Similarly, at Boyland Hall near Long Stratton, rents declined from £3,673 in 1877 to £2,224 ten years later, and £1,611 in 1896.[3] Therefore the position of farmers gradually began to improve and by 1900 tenants were usually fully compensated for the fall in agricultural prices by rent reductions.

During this deepening phase of the depression tenants were in a strong bargaining position. At a time when landowners were not themselves farmers, it was realised too late that even a non-paying tenant was preferable to an empty farm. Existing tenants were able to negotiate realistic rent levels by threatening to vacate their holdings. Thomas Handley gave notice to the Traffords of Wroxham to quit his holding on their West Walton estate, and was offered a reduction in rent from £55 to £44 a year.[4] His annual rent on eighteen acres rented in Elm was also reduced, from £46 to £36. Prospective tenants were able virtually to dictate their own terms for taking on farms at favourable rents. To make matters even more difficult for landowners, there was always the risk of the 'asset-stripping' tenant or 'landskinner' who went from farm to farm exhausting the soil by failing to replenish it with manures and fertilizers. Farms changed hands with increasing frequency, and old loyalties were severed.

Figures published by the government illustrate the serious decline in rentals, but the situation was even more gloomy than national published figures suggest. For one thing, these fail to emphasise the regional diversity of the depression, in that stock-rearing areas situated near to growing conurbations in the north-west suffered relatively lightly in comparison with the arable counties of the east of England. Statistics on national rental decline also tend to underestimate the true extent of additional rebates, remissions, allowances and mounting rent arrears. In Norfolk the Chamber of Agriculture's figures, based on actual *received* rents rather than contractual ones, recorded a rental decline of 25-30 per cent on the best lands and 40-60 per cent on medium soils. The position was even more burdensome on estates situated on very light land, on poor heavy soil and on some of the fenlands where 'no rents can be obtained, there being numerous instances of farms abandoned, and of farms let rent free.' The fate of marginal landowners in Norfolk at the turn of the century was observed by Rider Haggard:

> Much of the light soil around Swaffham that in the prosperous days commanded 7/6 an acre, was practically derelict. ... The landlords were much crippled and many of them, after paying charges, taxes, tithe and repairs, etc, had only their shooting rents on which to live.[5]

It should be noted, however, that less than one quarter of the county was of poor land and subject to these dramatic falls in rent, and so the extreme difficulties of the marginal landowners were not typical of all landowners. The sense of poverty in the depression period was often purely relative to the lavish spending power to which some landowners had become accustomed during the 'Golden Years'. There can be no denying that the depression formed a convenient excuse for those in straitened circumstances when, in many cases, the true cause of their financial difficulties was earlier extravagance or inefficient management. And certainly landowners and farmers alike had a vested interest in convincing the government that times were extremely hard, for the most severe depression years coincided with the imposition of Death Duties and active campaigns for land reform. The more influential landowners, often those upon whom the strain of depression bore less heavily, tended to be especially vociferous in proclaiming the seriousness of their plight. But no Norfolk landowner escaped significant curtailment of agricultural income. Even the Earl of Leicester, with his 43,000 acre Holkham estate, eventually began to feel the pinch, for his gross annual rental fell from £51,908 in 1880 to £31,393 in 1900.[6] To the average landowner in Norfolk during the closing decades of the nineteenth century, landed property had become a liability, for the pressures of ownership and management increased while revenue from the land fell drastically, sometimes disastrously.

Effects of depression on living standards

In the earlier years of the depression, during the 1870s and 1880s, landowners assumed that expedient economies would see them through what they expected to be a temporary decline in their fortunes. There was often some reduction in building, maintenance and repairs both on the estate and to the mansion, and occasionally the park was let for grazing. They restricted consumption and placed restraints on household expenditure. Some of the carriage horses were sold, visits to London became less frequent, and greenhouses were closed as the gardening staff was reduced.

Often the first signs of more severe financial embarrassment were sales of valuables from the mansion, or the contents of the wine cellar. There

Figure 1 The Library at Diddington Hall from the sale catalogue of 1911. A sale from the Library had realized £110,000 two years earlier.

19

were many such sales. Vendors were not keen to advertise their difficulties, disposing of their treasures through discreet intermediaries or sending them to the great London salerooms labelled 'The Property of a Gentleman'. One of the most important of these sales comprised books from the Didlington Library, sold by Lord Amherst in 1909. The proceeds amounted to £57,592 plus an extra £52,000 for the Caxtons bought en bloc privately prior to the sale,[7] a massive sum in the years before the First World War (Fig.1). The financial circumstances which necessitated this sale cannot be attributed directly to the agricultural depression, for defalcation by a London solicitor and subsequent loss of investment income forced a very severe retrenchment upon Lord Amherst. However, if his agricultural assets had been more profitable at the time the crisis would have been contained more easily. In the 1860s, the Fountaines had considerably extended Narford Hall to the designs of William Burn. Twenty years later they were selling part of the treasures put together by one of the greatest collectors of the eighteenth century, Sir Andrew Fountaine (1676-1735). The 565 lots of Maiolica and Limoges enamels sold in 1884 were part of one of the most distinguished European collections of its kind, and the collection of Palissy ware is considered to have been the finest in existence, more important even than the collection in the Louvre Museum in Paris. The total proceeds of the four-day sale amounted to an enormous £81,112. In the same year there was a further sale from Narford of 870 lots of engravings, etchings and drawings (Fig.2). One of the most outstanding sales of the interwar years took place in New York in 1932, when illustrated manuscripts from Blickling Hall were auctioned. These were proclaimed as 'the most valuable and interesting to be sold by auction since 1912'. Of the thirty-five manuscripts and 133 books, a Psalter of the eighth century fetched 23,000 dollars and Giovani's Boccaccio - described as 'the most important early illustrated book ever sold by auction' - sold for 45,000 dollars. These were sales from amongst Norfolk's more famed collections. For the hard-pressed smaller gentry, results were less rewarding. In 1903 George Holmes sold thirty-eight pictures from Brooke Hall, among which were several from the Norwich School of Painting, less acclaimed in those days. Two John Sell Cotmans, *The Storm, Yarmouth Beach* and *The Windmill*, sold for £257 5s and £262 10s respectively. A couple of paintings by John Crome, *A Heath Scene: Sun Breaking out After a Storm* and *Old Bathing House*, fetched £136 10s and £273.

CATALOGUE

OF

THE CELEBRATED

FOUNTAINE COLLECTION

OF

MAJOLICA,

HENRI II. WARE, PALISSY WARE,

NEVERS WARE,

LIMOGES ENAMELS,

Carvings in Ivory, Hone Stone and Rock Crystal, Greek and
Roman Coins, Ancient Armour, &c., &c.,

Removed from Narford Hall, Norfolk:

𝕎𝔥𝔦𝔠𝔥 𝔴𝔦𝔩𝔩 𝔟𝔢 𝔖𝔬𝔩𝔡 𝔟𝔶 𝔄𝔲𝔠𝔱𝔦𝔬𝔫, 𝔟𝔶

MESSRS. CHRISTIE, MANSON & WOODS,

AT THEIR GREAT ROOMS,

8 KING STREET, ST. JAMES'S SQUARE,

On MONDAY, JUNE 16, 1884,

And following days,

AT ONE O'CLOCK PRECISELY.

May be viewed Friday and Saturday preceding, and Catalogues
had, at Messrs. CHRISTIE, MANSON and WOODS' Offices, 8, *King Street,*
St. James's Square, S.W.

Figure 2. The Catalogue of the Fountaine Collection Sale, 1884.

21

Many other estates in Norfolk were able to increase estate revenues by letting the shooting, which was normally over the poorer land where rents dropped most severely during the depression. Lord Walsingham told Rider Haggard that owners in the vicinity of Merton were enabled to 'muddle along' only on the proceeds of the sporting amenities of their land. 'Indeed the majority of owners in that district would receive no advantage from their land were it not for its suitability to the purposes of game rearing'. Rider Haggard spoke also to Edward Bagge of Gaywood, enquiring how landlords managed to survive under the difficult conditions prevailing. He explained: 'They let the sporting rights and live in the housekeeper's room.'[8]

An immediate source of finance was timber sales, and extensive felling took place on many estates. In some cases hundreds of years' growth fell to the axes of timber merchants - symbolic, perhaps. At Burlingham, for instance, in 1901 fifty-seven oaks, ash and a sweet chestnut were sold, including two especially fine oaks. This was but one of many such sales. Around 1740 Robert Marsham had started plantations at Stratton Strawless, an estate which was renowned for its beeches, Scots pine, silver fir, spruce, oaks, hornbeam and Spanish chestnuts.[9] When the estate was put on the market in 1918 the government requisitioned the timber prior to the auction.

As their position worsened more drastic measures were introduced, such as shutting down the house in order to dispense with household staff. Sir Lawrence Jones of Cranmer Hall recounted his memories of the 1890s when:

One by one, the laundry was closed, the footman left, and after him the groom; Mr Basham retired from the garden and was not replaced.

The Jones family, before letting Cranmer Hall and taking refuge abroad, had employed a butler, housekeeper, footman, cook and kitchenmaid, three housemaids, two laundry maids, two nurses, a coachman and groom, four gardeners, two gamekeepers, two woodmen and two estate carpenters. Cutting down on staff expenses was an effective means of economising. After the First World War the much discussed 'servant problem' resulted in a general reduction in the number of servants employed, but even so in 1920 the wage bill at Boyland Hall amounted to more than £1,200 a year: the indoor staff were paid £393, the coachman £51, gardeners £369, gamekeeper £150, carpenter £101 and chauffeur £147 (Fig.3).

By leaving their homes to take up residence elsewhere, landowners not only saved the cost of servants and of maintenance expenses but also they were able to escape the financial responsibilities and expectations associated with their position as local dignitaries. In 1875 the Rolfe family of Heacham

Figure 3. The household of Lady Ffolkes of Hillington in the 1860s. Even the households of widows were large at this date.

were forced by contracting income to let the house and set sail for South Africa. Eustace Rolfe stayed there fore eighteen months, and later took up residence in Naples. He had imagined that he would live cheaply abroad for a couple of years and would then be able to return to Norfolk and live as his father had. The family pined to be back at Heacham but economic circumstances never improved sufficiently for this to become possible.[10]

If all else failed, the hall, park and farms were doomed to fall into a state of neglect. Ketton Cremer described how Felbrigg was allowed to deteriorate during the ownership of his great-uncle Robert Ketton between 1872 and 1924;

> Repairs were neglected, to farmhouse and farm buildings and cottages alike. Land was undrained, watercourses became choked, nothing was done to drives and roads. ... Damp began to soak everywhere through the roofs. The shrubbery grew into an entanglement and the lawn into a hayfield.

Although the china and some of the best furniture and plate and books were sold, this did not bring in enough money to encourage the owner to maintain Felbrigg, the estate in which he had once taken such pride. 'He just lost heart.'[11]

The Deepening of depression in the interwar years

Although farmers' incomes improved during the first two decades of the twentieth century, slight increases in landowners' rental income were more than offset by escalating maintenance costs and taxation increases. When wartime profits encouraged the aspirations of farmers to own farms themselves, land prices increased sufficiently to encourage landowners to sell. The joys as well as the rewards of landownership had diminished, and this long-awaited opportunity to unload estates was taken with some relief. But recovery was short-lived. Easy profits made by farmers during the war held until May 1920, after which there was a sustained fall in agricultural prices as the British market was again inundated with imports. Agricultural prices, which had trebled between 1912 and the summer of 1920, fell to less than twice the pre-war level by the end of 1921 and continued to fall.

This time landowners did not delude themselves that the returned depression was of a temporary nature. The crisis during the 1920s was international in its aspect. Although both agriculture and manufacturing industry were affected, farming prices were especially vulnerable because the depression coincided with the accumulation of large stocks of cereals in Europe as a result of over-production and record harvests. The arable areas such as Norfolk and the eastern counties were again hit first and the most seriously. In 1920 wheat had fetched an average of 18s.10d a cwt. Within three years the price had halved to 9s.10d a cwt. After some strengthening of prices until 1926 there were further falls to a nadir of 4s.10d a cwt in 1934, only one quarter of the 1920 price. The interwar collapse of prices was far more dramatic than that suffered during the nineteenth century agricultural depression. The earlier depression was alarming in its time but it was more gradual and less severe than that of the interwar period: the wheat price in 1894 had still been thirty-nine per cent of the 1873 price.

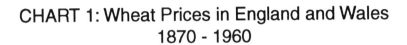

CHART 1: Wheat Prices in England and Wales 1870 - 1960

Shillings per cwt.

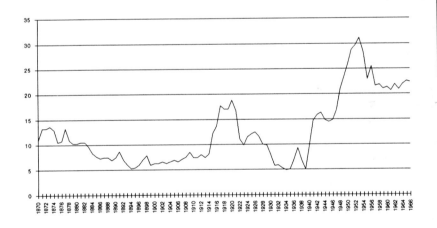

Source: "A Century of Agricultural Statistics", Ministry of Agriculture, Fisheries and Food", (1968), Table 36, p. 82.

Norfolk was affected especially severely, for although the arable area was reduced during the 1920s, in the interwar period East Anglia was the only region in Britain in which the area of arable land consistently exceeded that of pasture. On the poorer soils in Norfolk the expenses of owning land were again greater than the returns in the form of rent. Cases were reported of owners who not only allowed tenants to farm rent free but who also subsidised their tenants' farm deficits. Lord Walsingham recalls what he describes as 'the hungry thirties', when rents on the brecklands of the Merton estate were often not collected. By 1940 it had 4,000 acres in hand, 'the tenants having flit in the night unable to face their farm workers whom they could not pay'.

In those especially difficult years between the wars, every effort had to be made to reduce labour costs on farms. Land was left undrained and uncleaned, fields were uncultivated, repairs to implements postponed, and farm buildings allowed to become dilapidated. The policy was necessarily short sighted for land allowed to become derelict would need expensive reclamation at a later date, but with costs much higher than rental income landowners had no option but to witness the deterioration of their asset. Henry Williamson described the condition of Old Castle Farm at Stiffkey as it was when he purchased it in 1937:

> The lane or road leading to the buildings was all water, and the yard we looked into seemed nearly three feet in mud. Flint walls were broken down, every gate was decayed or fallen to pieces. ... There were no drains to the yards or stables or cow houses, gutters were fallen, the road was impassable. ... The larger dykes ... were full of reeds and rotting vegetation.[12]

The dilapidated state of Old Castle Farm is hardly surprising in view of the fact that it had been let in the 1930s at £100 a year, from which the landlord paid tithes of £80, drainage rates of £18, and income tax of £22, so that expenses exceeded income by £20 a year, without any account being taken of management expenses and the most minimal repairs.

Edward Lee Warner's report in 1930 on the condition of Wormegay was no more favourable. This property of 1,200 acres was an outlying portion of the Walsingham Abbey estate. He wrote:

I walked round the dykes, over Shoulder Warren to Pentney Mill and back along the Nar to High Bridge. That further end of the property by Pentney Drove is in a bad mess and all the smaller ditches seem well choked. Some of the fields were a mass of dead nettle, thistle and willow-herb, and appeared to have been let run wild for two or three years.

By 1930 rents on Wormegay brought in an income of £912, while drainage, rates, tithe, dole, repairs, management costs, Land Tax and Schedule B tax cost £878 a year. The net income was therefore £34, and the agent stated that he was having difficulty collecting the rents, and some were in arrears. He expected the estate in 1931 to be making a dead loss of at least £200 per annum after Michaelmas. This was at a time when the agricultural depression was deepening but had not yet bottomed out. George Lee Warner was pessimistic about the chance of finding a purchaser for Wormegay, for there was little demand for farms. An offer of £1,500 plus expenses was made for the 1,200 acre estate by a potato farmer whose land bordered the Wormegay land. Lee Warner was disheartened by the situation and decided to accept the offer, for, as he pointed out:

The time of good offers has gone for an indefinite period. There is no recovery in sight. ... Let us take the miserable offer and be done with it. Would any of us accept Wormegay as a gift? Not I for one.[13]

The Will to Survive

For the smaller owner with no outside income, erosion of values and disintegration of his asset in land was indeed a disheartening experience. For a large minority the depression was a disastrous time from which they would never recover. But for some the difficult times merely necessitated a certain amount of retrenchment and stimulated new attitudes towards commercialisation and greater efficiency. It was a period which forced essential readjustments before long-term benefits were gained and the transition was slow and often painful. Greater business acumen was required in the management of a large estate and heirs, at colleges such as Cirencester, learnt how to gain enhanced efficiency from the land through improved techniques and scientific application. Survival depended partly on exploiting an estate's full potential.

More vital to survival, however, was adequate income from outside sources with which to subsidise an estate through the lean years of depression. This was emphasised repeatedly, and many landowners became convinced that the wise course was to employ an efficient manager and to create extra revenue by pursuing a career in the fields of business, commerce or the professions. While retaining close personal involvement in their estates they could in this way provide an assured financial backing so essential when estate income declined. In 1937 Burke's **Landed Gentry** took up this point:

> In most cases where families are still able to retain their land they do so because they have resources other than their rent-rolls on which to rely and many men hold acres for sentimental reasons at some expense to themselves largely out of what they earn in various walks of life.

So long as acreages were reasonably extensive few Norfolk brewers, bankers, solicitors and businessmen were forced to sell their estates in the interwar period if they were determined to retain them. This, of course, is the salient point. Retention of estates depended often upon the will to survive.

How can one identify the rationale which finally led to the irrevocable decision to sell? While some were enthralled with country pursuits, estate management and local politics, others quietly tolerated the tedium and remoteness of country life and assumed the role of country squire only so long as this was justified by the social and financial recompense involved. However, there were many landowners who endured the onslaughts of politicians and the constraints forced upon their living standards in order to preserve the heritage of future generations. For these the long phase of depression entailed a determined fight to retain old traditions and to preserve family estates, seeing themselves as one link in a long chain of historic descent. A respect amounting almost to reverence for the land of his forefathers was expressed by Lord Hastings in 1936:

> It is the land which comes first, the land which has to be handed down to the succeeding generation in proper condition. ... It always remains the land which is important. The land comes before the person.[14]

Lord Hastings was speaking at a 'Festival of the Land' in the year which commemorated 700 years of unbroken possession of the Melton Constable estate by the Astley family.

To part with the family home entailed a significant break with the past and was a source of sadness to many vendors, however prudent the decision. Lord Ferrers recalled 'the terrible wrench, the feeling of losing family roots', which he experienced in 1954 when the last of the Ferrers' land in Leicestershire had to be sold. By the date of the sale the estate had been reduced to 1,700 acres, from a total in 1873 of 8,000 acres. Lord Ferrers' father, who had made strenuous efforts over a long period to find a buyer who would preserve the family mansion, died the night before the auction.[15]

Changes in landownership

In spite of sacrifice and struggle many estates changed hands or were broken up or greatly reduced in size as a result of almost continuous agricultural depression after 1880. For the minor gentry and the squires retrenchment alone in face of contracting income was inadequate to ensure survival, and sales were sometimes inevitable. Often burdened with debt at the onset of depression and seldom able to call upon financial reserves, the squires were too vulnerable to economic misfortune to withstand a long period of income decline. In 1880 there were thirty-two Norfolk estates comprising 2,000-3,000 acres; a hundred years later only five of these had retained 1,000 acres in the ownership of their original families. Although at first sight it seems that many owners are still established upon their original estates, in fact constant sales have so whittled away their landholdings that they retain only the hall and park and a few farms.

A distinction, however, must be clearly drawn between the minor gentry and the larger landowners, who have shown a greater propensity for survival. The large estates were able to contend with agricultural depression because they had sufficient land to be able to sell off considerable portions and still retain a viable economic unit. With the proceeds of sales they could ensure an income from alternative investment, reduce debts and then improve their land to revitalise the estate. In 1884 there were eleven estates in Norfolk comprising 10,000 or more acres. One hundred years later eight of these had been retained in the hands of the same families.[16] Some, but not all, had been considerably reduced in size, and there have been further sales since 1984.

The greatest revolution in landownership this century has been the extension of owner occupation of farms. This was a vital development, especially in the early interwar period, when six million acres of land formerly farmed by tenants (about one fifth of the cultivated area of Britain) was bought for owner occupation. Possibly this added to the distress of the interwar period. Many farmers who bought land at inflated prices between 1917 and 1922 were saddled with heavy mortgage payments, which some were unable to meet when the lean years came upon them. In difficult seasons a landlord had often been willing to defer or remit rent, but mortgagees were less helpful. In the 1930s it was stated that the banks owned virtually half of Norfolk as a result of foreclosure.

Loss of Country Houses

One sequel to the estate sales was the loss of many country houses in Norfolk. The landowners' faith in the future of agriculture and their traditional way of life declined, and interest in maintaining their houses faded with it. With agricultural incomes so curtailed in the interwar period, landowners shrank from the financial liabilities of essential repairs and maintenance to their country homes. Pessimism over the future prospects for agriculture led to abandoned life styles and uninhabited halls. In 1936 the *Eastern Daily Press* referred to 'the growing host of people who have been watching with anxious eyes and with sad hearts the diminishing number of beautiful country houses and estates that time and taxation have left unspoilt in the hands of enlightened and public spirited owners.'[17]

The Second World War hastened the demise of many country houses. Some were occupied by troops or evacuees. Much damage was done in the process and they were returned in such a state of disrepair that owners had neither the will nor the finance to refurbish them. Heacham Hall did not survive the war - it was destroyed by fire when occupied by the army in 1941. Many houses were under military occupation, including Shotesham, Necton and Woodrising. Weeting Hall was a training centre for immigrants and later a military Headquarters. Parts of Stow Bardolph, Woodbastwick and Cranmer were used for convalescent homes for the Forces. The Airforce took over Bylaugh, and Stratton Strawless became an RAF headquarters.

30

Sprowston Hall was the base of the GOC Eastern Command, and Did-lington before D-Day was General Dempsey's Headquarters. Some of these houses suffered few ill effects, but the old pattern of residential landowning was interrupted by the war and in several cases never resumed.

In the immediate postwar years the election of a Labour Government, petrol rationing, electricity cuts, coal shortage and lack of servants eroded the pleasures of country house living and removed the incentive to battle against dry rot, or to modernise nineteenth century installations of plumbing and heating. Most of Morton Hall was pulled down in 1952. The house, dating from 1599, was described by its last owner, Mr John Berney, as a lovely house which, although retaining some of its charm, was in poor shape by 1952 and was unmanageable in size, having twenty-six bedrooms. Many Norfolk landowners were faced with a similar decision - whether to endeavour to restore, staff and heat a great mansion or to demolish or sell it and move to a more practical home. Honingham Hall had been bequeathed after the Second World War to Dr Barnardo's, who built a new hostel in Norwich and sold the hall in 1964. By this time at least £50,000 was needed to make the place reasonably habitable. In 1966 the Ministry of Housing and Local Government decided they could not confirm a preservation order for Honingham Hall, for they considered that on economic grounds it was not worth preserving, and the hall was demolished. Hunstanton Hall was sold in 1951 and turned into flats. The following year the main block was gutted by fire. The fine old staircase, one of the showpieces of the Hall, was reduced to charred wood, and the fire ravaged the Plantaganet block and one of the Stuart wings. By good fortune the Henry VII gatehouse, the Jacobean drawing room, the Priest's Room and the east Stuart wing survived (Fig.8). John Harris mourned the loss of such halls as the result of fire, neglect and demolition:

> The twenties, thirties, late forties and early fifties are black decades in our architectural history. Month after month occurred that dreadful series of demolition and smash-ups that destroyed some of the greatest works of British art and endeavour.[18]

Considering only the 106 large Norfolk estates studied in this book, halls demolished or considerably reduced in size by 1939 included Costessey Park, Weston, Elmham, Congham, West Harling and Marham. Since the war destruction, ruination or substantial demolition have sealed the fate of halls on the estates of Boyland, Brooke Hall, Burlingham, Bylaugh, Castle Rising, Cranmer, Didlington, Feltwell, Garboldisham, Haveringland, Heacham, Hillington, Honingham, Hunstanton, Morton, Necton, Weeting, Woodbastwick, Wretham and Wroxham.[19]

Weston, Bylaugh and Haveringland provide good case studies. Weston Longville was the property of the Custance family for exactly two centuries, having been bought in 1726 by John Custance, a Norwich cloth merchant. His grandson, John, married Frances Beauchamp-Proctor of Langley Park in 1778. Three years later the couple took up residence in the handsome newly-built Georgian mansion named Weston House. The estate was put up for sale in September 1926. The following February, on instructions of the executors of the late Colonel F.H. Custance, the contents of the house were sold in 1335 lots. The sale included rare and valuable antique furniture, sixty-two oil paintings and engravings, and an extensive library of books. The family portraits were specifically excluded from the sale, some to be auctioned anonymously in London by Christie's, including Benjamin West's portrait of Mr and Mrs John Custance, painted in 1778 to commemorate their marriage (Fig.4). Later the house was pulled down and in May 1927 a demolition sale took place, when interior fittings auctioned included exquisite Adam mantlepieces, an Adam staircase and ornamental ceilings and friezes, some of which were later re-installed in America. The *Eastern Daily Press* wryly commented:

The stately homes of England such as the Adam period threw up come nowadays into the white elephant category.[20]

Bylaugh Hall was perhaps the grandest Victorian house in Norfolk. Parson Armstrong from East Dereham noted in his diary the sumptuousness of its contents and the grand life-style of its occupants, the Evans-Lombes. By 1950 Bylaugh Hall had been gradually reduced to a ruin, after delays in awarding a preservation order. The *Eastern Evening News* described this once splendid mansion as a 'magnificent shell':

In its former glory, Bylaugh had been more of an Italian palazzo than an English country house, with its fine columns, panel-carved ceilings and white and gold modelling. Now it stands open to the sky, roof gone, and windowless. Yet trailing ivy and thorn cannot mask the magnificence of the proud ruin that has stood desolate for so long.[21]

Figure 4. The marriage portrait painted by Benjamin West in 1778 of John Custance and his wife, famed as 'Squire and Mrs Custance' in Parson Woodforde's *Diaries*. Sold in London by Christie's in 1927, and by 1934 was in the possession of the Nelson Museum, Kansas City Reproduced by courtesy of The Nelson-Atkins Museum of Art, Kansas City, Missouri (Nelson Fund) 34-77.

Figure 5. Felbrigg Hall. Robert Windham Ketton-Cremer, the last squire of Felbrigg, saw the estate restored by his father and left it to the National Trust on his death in 1969.

Figure 6. The west front of Didlington Hall in 1911. General Sir Miles Dempsey's headquarters in the Second World War, it was demolished in 1950.

Figure 7. Hunstanton Hall, home of the Le Strange family from 1310 to 1950. The gateway was crowned with their arms and supporters.

Figure 8. Hunstanton Hall: The Jacobean Drawing Room which survived the fire of 1952.

Figure 9. Lexham Hall before restoration.

Figure 10. Lexham Hall after restoration in 1948.

Figure 11. Craftsman relaying lead at Melton Constable Hall in 1990.

Figure 12. Gunton Hall: the Matthew Bretingham wing, derelict in the 1970s.

Figure 13. Gunton Hall after restoration.

The Haveringland Hall Estate belonged to a second branch of the Fellowes family. Haveringland's large house, the third on the site, had been built in stone, unusually in Norfolk, during the early 1840s by Edward Fellowes (later the first Lord de Ramsey). When the family concentrated its activities on their other property in Huntingdonshire (Ramsey Abbey) the estate was sold to Viscount Rothemere in 1927. Until the war, Haveringland Hall was surrounded by extensive park and woodlands, with a magnificent lake and a stately chestnut avenue. A few years later the place ws derelict. In June 1949 the *Eastern Daily Press* reported:

The war brought the vast encroachment of a modern airfield which levelled the ground to each familiar landmark. ... A perimeter track replaced the wall that had encircled the estates. ... Three years have passed, and today all is still. Grass grows in runways. The Nissen huts

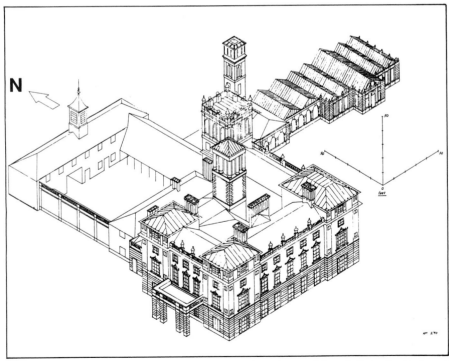

Figure 14. Haveringland Hall from a line drawing by Alan Mackley. Built in the 1840s and 1850s, to Edward Blore's designs for the Fellowes family, it was demolished in 1946.

stand gaping and derelict. The Hall, which no man wants for a home, shorn as it is of its trees and gardens, is being demolished.[22]

Soon after the war ended, the hall was pulled down to make way for a caravan park. The victims of war included some of Norfolk's most notable estates.

This impression of loss and desolation is a constant theme in a review of landownership in the period 1870 to the 1950s. It was difficult to reconcile the desire to preserve traditional links within a family with the economic expediency of selling estates and homes which had become a liability. The repercussions of this conflict were expressed by Lord Crawford:

> In times of change two different impulses showed themselves. One was the impulse to preserve the established, beautiful and orderly things at all costs; the other was to sacrifice them for the sake of other over-riding values. It was a terrible thing in the life of any person when these two impulses came into direct and violent conflict.[23]

Optimism returned with the revival of agricultural prosperity in the late 1950s. A new generation of landowners deplored the philistine neglect and destruction of their family homes, the dispersal of their treasures throughout Europe and America, the felling of their finest trees at the hands of the land developers. Halls, unoccupied for many years, were modernised and refurbished, some saved at the eleventh hour from destruction. One wing of Lexham Hall, during the Second World War, had housed evacuees from Dr Barnado's homes and the remainder was used as a Royal Army Service Corps dump. On the estate, £5,000 worth of softwood trees were cut down. In 1946 William Foster bought the dilapidated house which he skilfully restored and added a handsome library (figs. 9 and 10). Trees and hedges and seven miles of shelter belts were planted.

Rather different restorations were those of Melton Constable and Gunton, two of the county's finest houses. A considerable acreage of the Melton Constable estate had been bought by G.W. Harrold in 1959, but the hall remained unoccupied. Seven years later the Historic Building Council expressed concern over the state of the building. The County Planning Committee reported that the hall was in need of extensive and urgent repairs. The house remained empty until bought in 1986 by a foreign investment company who stated that they were prepared to spend £3 million restoring the seventeenth century listed building to its former glory (fig.11). In the early nineteenth century Gunton Park had been one of the finest properties in Norfolk. After a protracted period of neglect the house became virtually derelict. But during the 1980s Kit and Sally Martin completed one of the most spectacular and ambitious country house rescues seen in Britain since the 1950s. The huge house was restored and 6,000 park trees were planted (figs. 12 and 13).

Few people nowadays seek a vast house with twenty or more bedrooms, and restorations like Gunton and Melton Constable divide the house and its ancillary buildings into smaller units to provide comfortable accommodation using all the benefits of modern building techniques, able to take full advantage of spectacular settings and grand facades. Because so much has already been lost, protection of our cultural heritage in this way has become invaluable.

NOTES

1. The Duke of Bedford, *A Great Agricultural Estate* (1897), p 181.

2. Royal Commission on Agricultural Depression, XVI, (1896) BPP Ag 32, Appendix C5: *Rentals and Outgoings on the Blickling Estate*

3. NRO IR 158, A, B45 & 46

4. NRO BRA 2067

5. Haggard, H. Rider, *Rural England*, Vol 11 (1902), pp 473-94.

6. Martins, S. Wade, *A Great Agricultural Estate at Work* (1980),Appendix 3, p 270

7. Colman and Rye Library, Norwich: Bound book of Sale Catalogues (uncatalogued)

8. Haggard, op cit

9. Cremer, R W Ketton, *A Norfolk Gallery* (1947), p 152

10. Berry, V., *The Rolfe Papers: The Chronicle of a Norfolk Family 1559-1908* (1979), p.129

11. Cremer, R.W. Ketton, *Felbrigg: The Story of a House* (1962) pp.273, 275, 283

12. Williamson, H., *The Story of a Norfolk Farm*, (1941) pp 37 and 87

13. NRO Lee Warner Box 24, no 9, 441 x 6: Family letters re. Wormegay

14. *Eastern Daily Press*, 9 September 1936

15. Perrott, R., *The Aristocrats* (1968), p 161

16. Barnes, P. "The Economic History of Landed Estates in Norfolk Since 1880", Unpublished PhD thesis, University of East Anglia 1984

17. *Eastern Daily Press*, 9 September 1936.

18. Strong et al, eds, *The Destruction of the Country House, 1875-1975*, (1974) Harris, J., "Gone To Ground"

19. Much of the above information is from Burke's and Savills' *Guide to Country Houses*, vol.111: East Anglia, ed. Hugh Montgomery-Massingberd (1981).

20. *Eastern Daily Press*, 4 May 1927.

21. *Eastern Evening News*, 1 December 1981.

22. *Eastern Daily Press*, 29 June 1949.

23. *The Times*, 11 October 1952.

Chapter Two
Indebtedness

Easy Money

Banks, insurance companies and private individuals favoured landed property as security for loans until the 1870s, and landowners had no difficulty in borrowing. Most seemed to have little compunction about mortgaging their estates to the hilt, and generally approached their London banks for a loan. Hoare's, Child's and Gosling's had built up a clientele of gentlemanly and aristocratic owners, and Coutt's and Drummond's were also favoured by landowners, while Wright's specialised in the affairs of the Catholic gentry.[1] By 1785 Hoares' total loans, advances and investments amounted to nearly £600,000. Furthermore, the country banks were willing to lend to local landowners: Gurneys opened their Norwich and Norfolk Bank in 1775; by 1825 they had lent £80,000 on mortgage.[2]

Although most large loans were negotiated through the banks, an enormous volume of small scale borrowing was essentially local and personal, arranged between relations and friends or through the family lawyer. At times the borrowing arrangements were of a somewhat *ad hoc* nature, as in the case of Sigismund Trafford's loan from John Calthrop. In a Release of Trafford's securities given on 4th February 1848, Calthrop informed W.James Green of Wroxham:

> When Mr Trafford borrowed the £1,000 of me in 1834 he came over to Lynn and the late Mr Coulton drew up a Bond for securing the same.

On my purchasing Stanhoe I was pressed for money and begged Mr Trafford to pay it off - He desired me to retain the sum due to me (which was then £1,200) and to borrow it for him elsewhere. He desired me to cancel the Bond which I did, and a receipt in full was sent to him by me.

I asked Messrs Unthank if they had a Client who would advance the money of Mr Trafford's Bond, but they had not, and to prevent disappointment I borrowed the money myself, and sent it to him, when he returned me the Note of Hand for £1,200 delivered by me to you, and which was the only Security in my possession or against Mr Trafford when I settled with you. I held no other.[3]

Another important source of borrowing was Insurance Companies, who placed a high proportion of their funds in landed property. In 1834 the Equitable Life Assurance Company had no less than £4 million allocated to mortgages, mostly secured on landed property.[4] The equivalent today would be in the region of half a billion pounds. By 1836 the Norwich Union had lent over £1 million in the form of loans secured on private property.

So long as sufficient disposable income remained to landowners after payment of interest charges, it seems that debt charges were accepted as normal outgoings on an estate. Often the charges, inherited along with the estate, had accumulated over several generations. Indeed, if disposable income was not too heavily absorbed by debt charges there was little incentive to reduce the debt commitment. After all, retrenchment alone was rarely effective as a means of reduction of large-scale debt - the only effective recourse would have been land sales. So debt remained a common feature of life for many of the Norfolk landed gentry, often sustained over long periods. It was after all the **proportion** of income devoted to servicing debts which was crucial, rather than the **size** of the debt. Mortgagees did not become apprehensive about their collateral until the fall in land values during the 1880s, by which time landowners' capacity to sustain debt charges was impaired by recent erosion of income. Whereas in the earlier part of the century incapacitating indebtedness was caused by debt charges rising more quickly than income growth, by the 1880s the position was different: disposable income actually fell, and continued to fall, until the margin between income and the level of debt charges narrowed precariously. This was a new, disturbing situation. Interest payments, bearable in earlier times, became impossibly burdensome as income shrank alarmingly. Many small owners had arrived at the point where sales became inevitable, delayed only by a falling land market in which mortgagees were loath to distrain. But from the 1880s they were forced to do so with the realisation that the downturn was no mere temporary phase, and that land was a fallible security.

Money had been too easy to borrow. But what had originally motivated excessive borrowing? Although debt was incurred for unprecedented and relatively unremunerative agricultural improvements, such as drainage and farm buildings, there were two main reasons for indebtedness. One was the payment of family settlements. The other reason was extravagance - spending large sums on house building or simply living beyond their means.

Family settlements

Family payments were a first charge on a settled estate, and often so demanding that the life tenant might receive for himself a mere fraction of the income of the estate with which to maintain it and provide for his family. Moreover, debts imposed by family settlements were cumulative from one generation to another. Mortgages as a means of discharging family obligations tended to proliferate because there was little legal restriction upon life-tenants' freedom to borrow for this purpose. These settlements were generally negotiated prior to the intended marriage of an heir, to provide maintenance for his wife if widowed, and for any children which the marriage might produce. As her jointure the widow would receive a yearly rent-charge payable throughout her widowhood. Such marriage settlements often contributed to later economic difficulties, for there was necessarily an element of actuarial uncertainty in calculating the commitment involved. The dowager might be widowed young and live for many years after the death of her husband. The marriage settlement of Cecil Thomas Molineux-Montgomerie of Garboldisham, for example, was negotiated in 1868 at the time of his marriage to Eleanor Lascelles. By this settlement about 1,000 acres of his 2,580 acre estate in Norfolk were charged with a jointure of £900 a year in favour of Eleanor (who was still living 63 years later), plus a sum of £12,000 for portions for the children of the marriage other than the eldest son.[5] This settlement was reasonable in relation to the family income in 1868 but it was not foreseen that rent rolls on the Garboldisham estate would contract sharply after 1880. Neither could it have been foreseen that considerable additional income from sugar plantations in Saint Kitts in the West Indies would fold under pressure of competition from subsidised continental beet sugar.⁶ In consequence, the estate became heavily indebted. Difficulties arose also on the Westacre estate, where actual income from rents and miscellaneous receipts amounted to £6,903 in 1896. This was a low rental from an estate of over 10,000 acres with a gross annual value of £9,917. Payments for the year, which included insurance, repairs, tithes, taxes, rates and wages, cost £3,776. But the balance of £3,127 would have been adequate had it not been for encumbrances in the form of debt repayment and annuities: interest on mortgages amounted to £2,571 plus £250 payable to a loan owing to Gurney & Co. and in addition an annuity was paid to Mrs Hamond which cost the estate £966. Fortunately, there was £1,221 in hand from the previous year's profits to cover these essential payments.⁷ But the year's accounts made gloomy reading.

Not all estates, however, could rely on such reserves, especially if overburdened by a large family. Estate finances had to be stretched sufficiently to provide portions for younger brothers and sisters. Portions were lump sums provided for the younger children on attaining majority, as compensation for not taking interests in the land. In some cases sons were provided with capital sums equal to their sisters' portions, possibly supported by annuities, but in other families sons received merely a sufficient sum to establish themselves in a profession or trade. When daughters married their portions were given as dowries - the more generous the dowry the greater the inducement to form an advantageous family alliance.

The Heacham estate was a prime example of overwhelming family encumbrances, reduced to insolvency by family obligations which eventually forced its sale in 1899. Charles Rolfe made his will during the 1860s, when the estate was bringing in £5,700 a year and was sufficiently profitable to provide an income for the eldest son, Eustace, £400 a year for the widow until she might remarry, £200 per annum to each of the three unmarried daughters reducing to £120 after marriage, and to each of the five younger sons £120 a year plus £1,000 to start a profession or business. There were also charges outstanding under Eustace's grandfather's will to Eustace's three surviving uncles and three surviving aunts: on the death or demand of these six people £3,000 would be due to each one or to their estate. When Charles Rolfe died in 1869 he left personal property amounting to £43,000 to the trustees for the upkeep of the estate.⁸ But a mis-wording in a codicil to his will led to a lawsuit which cost Eustace £2,558; and his step-mother negotiated a capital sum of £4,778 plus an income of £800 for life, instead of £400 a year until she remarried. In fact she lived for 38 years after Charles Rolfe's death, and she remarried four years after being widowed. Charles Rolfe's second marriage, of only eighteen months' duration, cost the family dear. A sharp decline in the income of the estate made it impossible to provide sufficient funds for all family charges and so the estate had to be sold.[9]

Most landowners who held heavily charged estates after 1880 were similarly encumbered by the provision of family charges which contributed to growing insolvency and mounting indebtedness.

Extravagance

Some estates were crippled because owners lived beyond their means, sometimes identifying with the circle surrounding the Prince of Wales. Edward Vll's mode of living demanded expenditure which only the very rich could match. It was a common interest in shooting which led to a friendship with the sixth Lord Walsingham, who was one of the finest shots in the country. He shot regularly at Sandringham and in turn entertained the Prince at Merton. The *Eastern Daily Press* referred to Lord Walsingham's 'charming and courteous personality, his kindness of heart, and his considerateness.'[10] Maybe his description in the same newspaper as 'perhaps the most versatile man in the Peerage' had some bearing on the fact that he was thrice married, and his great nephew recounts how 'his marital infidelities also were remarkable, in an age when infidelity was commonplace.'[11] But apart from his sporting and sexual prowess, Lord Walsingham had a serious side. He was an acknowledged authority on entomology, Director of the British Museum and High Steward of the University of Cambridge. As a scientist he was highly respected, but he seems to have lacked business acumen and financial judgement, and the present Lord Walsingham observes that his great uncle 'had a lordly view of entrepreneurial activity.' In 1870 he had succeeded to the Merton estate of 12,000 acres, which was flourishing and singularly free from debt. He also held a further 5,590 acres in Yorkshire, inherited through his mother, as well as 1,075 acres in Suffolk. The estimated aggregate annual value of all he inherited was £16,178.[12] In addition to these great agricultural estates he

Figure 15. Costessey Hall, showing the original Tudor house on the right, the early nineteenth century chapel and the vast linking block with its 130 feet tower built after 1827.

Figure 16. The Salon at Costessey in 1913, one of the lavishly furnished rooms added during the nineteenth century.

Figure 17: Shadwell Hall showing S.S. Teulon's expensive rebuilding of the late 1850s. Before the 1830s the Buxtons inhabited a modest Georgian house.

Figure 18. Many landowners enjoyed a fine and expensive stable of horses. These stables at Shadwell were designed by S.S.Teulon for Sir Robert Buxton.

owned Walsingham House in Piccadilly (now the site of the Ritz hotel) and the freehold of the valuable grounds surrounding the house. In 1876 his income from his Norfolk estates alone brought in £9,695, but these rentals began to slip alarmingly during the depression. Walsingham tried desperately to augment his dwindling resources, turning his great London house into a club, and speculating in railways 'from the local line, Thetford to Swaffham, all the way to South America' at a time when railway investment was declining. In spite of the failure of his speculations and his contracting agricultural income, he went on spending lavishly on the shoots at Merton and in entertaining the Prince of Wales' set. His accountants informed him that at Michaelmas 1890 the sum of £14,356 was outstanding.[13] By 1911 all the assets of any value which were not subject to settlement had been disposed of. When an over-lavish lifestyle was not tempered with the rational cutbacks dictated by the effects of agricultural depression, his insolvency, followed by exile abroad for the last seven years of his life, became inevitable.

Another instance of an estate denuded by lavish expenditure was Gunton. Under the third Lord Suffield the estate comprised some of the best farmed land in Norfolk and was renowned throughout the East of England. But his son by his first marriage, the fourth Lord Suffield, who inherited the estate in 1835, showed little interest in it except as a security for the Sun Insurance Company in order to provide him with a life annuity of £15,000. His extravagance and wilful neglect of his obligations over a period of twenty-four years impoverished the estate. Upon his death in 1859 he was succeeded by his half-brother, Charles, fifth Lord Suffield (1830-1914) who inherited an estate 'mortgaged to the eyebrows'. In the early years he made stringent efforts to put his estate on a sounder financial footing, but his zeal faded and by the 1880s he was living from the capital of the estate, with increasing ostentation regardless of the shrinkage of his agricultural income. Financial difficulties were evident from his reluctance to restore Gunton Hall after the fire of 1882 which gutted the central Matthew Brettingham block, comprising the State rooms - library, drawing room, dining room, billiard room and smoking room. Only about a third had been restored within five years, and even in 1911 this section of the house remained uninhabitable, with windows still unglazed. In spite of dwindling agricultural income, Suffield continued to entertain Prince Edward and his friends to shoots run on the extravagant lines essential for those who entertained them regularly. If even such wealthy men as Lord Walsingham reeled under the cost of keeping pace with the Prince of Wales' set, Lord Suffield must have strained the resources of his estate irredeemably. In 1904, at the age of seventy-four, he handed over to his eldest son - with the strongest family encouragement to do so. His Middleton estate in Lancashire, Vernon House in London and several other properties had already been sold. After his son succeeded further extensive sales were necessary. In 1919, 5,879 acres were sold for a total of £148,000. By 1939 there had been further land sales, reducing the original 11,828 acres (in 1880) to 3,000 acres.

Many landowners were lured by the dictates of fashion and the increasing complexities of country house life into executing renovations, extensions and rebuilding of their homes. The passion for improvements led to improvident spending on a lavish scale and contributed to mounting levels of debt. Costessey provides an instance of this. The Staffords had withdrawn, socially and economically, from industrial interests in the Midlands and had re-invested much of this wealth in their estate at Costessey, near Norwich, with adverse effects on the prosperity of the family. Added to this misjudgment had been an extensive rebuilding of Costessey Hall, commenced in 1827 to designs by J. C. Buckler Thornbury, and continued by the ninth baron. The dining room of the original Elizabethan house led to a new library and drawing room, flanked by a picture gallery 108 feet long. At the western end of this gallery was erected a great tower, 130 feet high, enhanced by pinnacles and clustered windows (fig.15). No expense had been spared in the construction of this magnificent house. The bricks were cast in special moulds, no fewer than a thousand moulds being required to supply the various enrichments of design. The St Amand Room, adjoining the magnificently fitted state apartments, displayed oak panelling, canopy and chimney-piece brought from the dismantled Abbey of St Amand, near Rouen. The whole house was impressively furnished. In the salon was a crimson Turkey carpet, thirty-five by twenty feet, upon which stood ebonised Florentine cabinets, Louis XV commodes, a Louis XVI writing table and a Bechstein seven octave grand piano. Around the room were twelve gilt-frame chairs of exquisite workmanship and a further pair of gilt-frame chairs with spring seats and stuffed backs covered in fine needlework portraying the Royal Arms and Jerningham crest. There were two walnut and amboyna-wood china cabinets, and a pair of Cloisonné enamel vases decorated with birds, trees and flowers. The room was lighted with a twenty-three light cut glass and crystal chandelier (fig.16). To adorn the whole house with furniture of such magnificence entailed considerable expenditure, yet in spite of declining agricultural income Lord Stafford continued to entertain lavishly until his death in 1884, when he died childless. In 1920, in the van of country house destruction, Costessey Hall was demolished. At the demolition sale items were knocked down for whatever price could be exacted from the bidders. The beautiful St Amand room, Lady Stafford's boudoir, was sold in situ, with 180 panels and delicately carved friezes, mouldings, skirtings, chimney-piece and over-mantle, the oak floor as laid, and the twelve-panelled oak door with carved frame and linings, also the heavily timbered ceiling. This fetched £350. The moulded timber ceiling of the armour room, sixty-one feet by eighteen feet and emblazoned with crests brought in £30. The interior of the historic oak panelled chapel, with altar and two family pews was sold for £175.

The nineteenth century was an era of conspicuous display and extravagance, and prodigal house improvements reflected the exhibitionist trend of the time. Shadwell Park, near Thetford, was a modest Georgian house, transformed by the Buxtons into a residence of monumental impressiveness, to designs by Blore in 1840, with major additions between 1855 and 1860 by Teulon. The extension had a vast oak-panelled hall fifty-five by fifty-three feet, lit by a traceried rose window with stained glass panels of noted musicians, and a handsome mullioned window (fig.17). A minstrels' gallery was added, as was a new drawing room, billiard room, large and small dining rooms, study and boudoir with panelled dado and carved wood chimney-piece. Of equal magnificence was the new oak sitting room, the south entrance hall, and the library which commanded a fine view of the lake which was enlarged to thirty acres with cascade, dell and boat house. This was building on an extraordinary scale for an old family of Norfolk baronets with an essentially modest income. The 11,000 acre estate was situated on the brecklands, poor agricultural land, and although the Buxtons also inherited property in Wiltshire their income in the earlier nineteenth century was only £8,000 a year.[14] Extravagant building ventures had depleted their resources and, not surprisingly, with the onset of agricultural depression the Buxtons found themselves in financial difficulties and Shadwell Park had to be sold in 1898. The estate was bought by Mr John Musker, who demonstrated that, in spite of its siting on poor breck land, the estate could indeed become a viable proposition when ample additional finances were invested. The splendid stable buildings erected by the Buxtons were extended and a fine stud of horses established on six model bloodstock stud farms, containing 171 loose boxes, two stallion boxes, two

Figure 19. The acme of late-nineteenth century country house existence, the entertainment of King Edward V11. He is seen here at Quidenham Hall in 1909 with his hosts, the Earl and Countess of Albemarle (he is first left back row, she seated second left).

Figure 20. Country House pursuits: Sir Edward and Lady Preston boating on the lake at Beeston St. Lawrence Hall in July 1887.

grooms' houses and exercise yards (fig.18). The scale of the enterprise was probably unequalled in England at the time. Between 1900 and 1903 forty-one horses from the Melton Studs won prize money of £52,160 in eighty-three races.

Lynford Hall was also situated on poor breckland. The gross annual value of the 7,000 acre estate in 1873 was only £2,736. It had been bought with the proceeds of wealth amassed by a rich English merchant in Lisbon, his fortune being inherited by Mr Lyne Stephens, who was said to have paid £133,000 for the estate and who expended further an incredible £145,000 to build the hall in 1858, designed by William Burn. The reception rooms of this new house were seventeen feet high, finished and decorated in a most elaborate and costly style. The walls of the forty-three foot dining room were decorated in embossed and gilt leather with a panelled oak dado, and the panelled ceiling was enhanced with coats of arms. Equally lavish were the sixty foot long library, the drawing room, billiard room and smoking room. A private gas works was built to supply the mansion and water was supplied from a deep well by steam pumps. The inherited fortune of Lyne Stephens may have been adequate to finance the cost of buying an estate and building a great house, but the income from the estate was too meagre to sustain its upkeep. The estate was sold in 1895 by order of the Judge in the Chancery Division of the High Court.

Many halls in Norfolk were renovated or rebuilt during the nineteenth century, partly because life styles changed. The coming of the railway age made estates more accessible, and lavish shooting parties were organised (fig.19). Each guest would bring his own retinue of staff, so big servants' wings were added to accommodate extra servants. New kitchens were added, from which were produced the formal dinner of eight courses which was expected on such occasions. The ladies might join the guns for a picnic lunch, but during inevitable intervals of inactivity they strolled in the gardens, which were replanned with terracing and balustrading, statues and fountains. No self-respecting Victorian landowner could feel his mission to improve had been accomplished unless he could instal or enlarge his lake. At Honingham Hall an extensive lake was constructed, and the park at Lynford was intersected by a small river with ornamental lakes in which were timbered islands. Shadwell was equipped with a lake of about thirty acres which (according to the 1898 Sale Catalogue) 'dotted with islands, profusely wooded, enhances to a superlative degree the picturesqueness of the surrounding scenery.' At Costessey the conservatory and terrace carried the buildings to the very edge of the new lake. These lakes were not merely ornamental, however, for they were utilised for fishing, wild-fowling, sailing or rowing.

Several Norfolk halls were transformed - or disfigured - with additions such as bow windows, heavy enclosed porchways, verandas and clock towers. The original Cranmer Hall dated from 1721, a pleasant manor house built in Norfolk red bricks. In his book *Georgian Afternoon* Sir Lawrence Jones describes how his grandfather 'entirely destroyed the agreeable face of the house by putting in plate glass windows, each divided by one clumsy horizontal bar, and by concealing the Georgian doorway behind a heavy enclosed brick porch, roofed with slates.' A bow window two stories high was thrown out 'on one side of this long-suffering facade' around which was built a veranda with cast-iron pillars, and a 'soaring gawky clock-tower' was added, supported by immense flying buttresses.

The 'improvements' at Honingham Hall made during the nineteenth century were equally deforming. Most of the Elizabethan east front was drastically altered and a mock gothic door added, and on the Georgian south front a pretty eighteenth century Venetian window was removed. Mock Jacobean windows and Victorian gables were added. Even relatively minor alterations such as this could cause embarrassing debts. Ronald Fellowes, who inherited the Honingham estate in 1894, never lived there, and the house was let until its sale by order of the mortgagees in 1935.

House building projects disfigured many Norfolk halls and saddled owners with debts which could prove so incapacitating that land sales became inevitable. This was regrettable, for those landowners who remained reasonably free of debts could endure income decline with relative equanimity. Had it not been for the burden of indebtedness and family encumbrances owners of 2,000 acres or more need never have been forced into land sales as a direct result of agricultural depression.

NOTES

1. Joslin, D.M., 'London Private Bankers, 1720-1785', *Economic History Review*, 2nd ser, Vll, 1954-5, pp 176-184

2. Bidwell, W.H., *Annals of an East Anglian Bank*, (1900), p 178

3. NRO TRAF 1041, 96 x 2. Settlement re Trafford Estates, Letter from Mr Calthrop of Stanhoe to James Green of Wroxham, from Paris 21 January 1848

4. Cannadine, D., 'Aristocratic Indebtedness in the Nineteenth Century: The Case Re-Opened', *Economic History Review*, 2nd ser, XXX (1977), p 636

5. NRO, Private papers in Collection 11277, shelf Q195a

6. Wilson, R.G., *Greene King: A Business and Family History* (1983) pp 51,158

7. NRO BIR 200/9, 398/ etc: Accounts of Estate of A. Hamond (decd)

8. Berry, V. *The Rolfe Papers: The Chronicle of a Norfolk Family 1559-1908* (1979), p 49

9. *Ibid*, pp 199, 206 and passim

10. *Eastern Daily Press*, 9 December 1919

11. Ruffer, J.G., *The Big Shots* (1977), Introduction by the present Lord Walsingham, p 8

12. Private information kindly provided by Lord Walsingham

13. NRO Walsingham MS 21554, l x 20, 21, 429 x 7

14. Girouard, M., *Life in the English Country House - A Social and Architectural History* (1978), p 95

Chapter Three
The Climate of Hostility

Only a parliament dominated by landowners could have passed the Corn Laws in 1815, introduced to protect farming after the Napoleonic Wars. As it happened the Corn Laws had little effect on the price of wheat to their repeal in 1846 because imported foreign corn was not significantly cheaper than home-grown nor in greater supply, and wheat acreages and yields both advanced to keep pace more or less with the increase in population. But the very existence of the Corn Laws illustrates the strength of the political power of the landed interest in parliament in the early nineteenth century. There was, however, an increasingly strong lobby of industrial and manufacturing interests who sought greater influence on the affairs of government, and who resented their political subjection to the predominant power of the landowners.

The Anti-Corn Law League was founded in Manchester in 1839 by a group who were dedicated to hastening the abolition of tariffs on imported goods, a process which had been gaining slow momentum since the 1820s. Based round Manchester, they represented the trading and manufacturing interests of the north of England whose costs of production were increased by payment of duties on imported raw materials. In an attempt to strengthen their political influence these advocates of free trade formed an influential pressure group, gaining support by focusing attention on the price of bread and moulding public opinion against a landowning class who, they insisted, were taxing the bread of the poor to enrich themselves. The tactics used by the Anti-Corn Law League were highly successful, their greatest achievement being to persuade the Whig Opposition to back them in their bid to remove tariffs from imports. In 1846 the Prime Minister, Robert Peel, himself the son of a manufacturer, introduced measures which were passed through parliament to repeal the Corn Laws.

The debate over the Corn Laws had suggested a real possibility that removing protection might ruin farmers. After 1846 there was indeed a short-lived depression in agriculture, but recovery soon followed and the 1850s and 1860s were the 'golden' years of agriculture. There was no sudden influx of foreign corn, for mainland Europe had a growing population and so needed her own grain. Furthermore, her agriculture was less efficient than in this country. America was not yet a rival, as it was both difficult and expensive to transport corn. However, by the 1870s railways improved and shipping developed. Imports of wheat began to flood in, carried in the new steamships, as the American prairies, Canada, Australia, the Argentine and Russia were rapidly opened up. In 1870 ten million quarters of wheat were imported, compared with half a million in the 1830s.

Following the success of the repeal of the Corn Laws, the campaign against the landed interest took the form of increased clamour to promote a more open land market by freeing the land from the legal trammels which inhibited its negotiability. Extremists even advocated a general redistribution of land. An ominous attack on private property was initiated in 1882 by Henry George, who affirmed that land should belong to the community as a whole. The 'land question' became an important issue in the political campaigns of the 1880s, featuring strongly in the country districts, where tenant farmers had been enfranchised in 1867 and agricultural labourers in 1884. But by the 1880s England was predominantly urban, and the urban voter was more concerned with the threat that protective tariffs would increase food prices and showed less interest in the land question. Stress on radical land reform was a political ploy which cost the Liberals the support of many a middle class owner of urban property, for there was fear that the principle of land nationalisation might be extended to common ownership of all land, including their own. In the event, constraints upon the purchasing of land were eased without recourse to solutions of the land reformers, for the Settled Land Act of 1882 removed most of the barriers to the sale of settled land, and the depression stifled enthusiasm for land purchase.

Agitation for reform of land tenure developed into a policy to discredit landlords, and anti-landlord campaigns were waged up and down the country. Criticisms of landowners became widespread and pronounced, focusing on the wealth they received from tenants as an unearned increment which underpinned their idleness and uselessness. Undoubtedly there was an element of truth in criticisms of land management and ownership, but allegations were deliberately exaggerated for political motives. Public opinion was being moulded against landlords as a class, and a climate of hostility was created. By the 1900s Lloyd George's speeches constantly attacked landlords, and his performances won him enthusiastic applause on the political platform. His appeals have been described as being 'all the louder and clearer for coming from a magnetic personality whose oratory and whose actions were uninhibited by regard for principle.'[1] Lloyd George's dynamism was directed against landed privilege with an intensity which, for a time, revitalised the Liberal party and fired the enthusiasm of crowds in the political arena.

Since 1860 nearly all tariffs had been reduced or removed and Britain was committed to a policy of Free Trade. But since the 1880s those same masters of industry who had pushed so determinedly for removal of tariffs had increasingly become concerned that the United States and Germany were catching up with our industrial capacity, and now some manufacturers began to demand a return to Protection to save industry from competition. In Birmingham Joseph Chamberlain campaigned for tariff reform and Imperial Preference. He was backed by the Conservatives and bitterly opposed by the Liberals who realised that 'cheap food' was a potential winner in an election campaign. They were correct in this, for in 1906 the Liberals won handsomely on a platform of Free Trade.

As Chancellor of the Exchequer, Lloyd George's attack on landed privilege continued in 1909 with 'The People's Budget', which proposed an increase in income tax, introduction of supertax at six (old) pence in the pound on incomes over £5,000, and increased death duties on estates over £5,000. His argument for taxing land was that revenue from it should pay for the social reform programme of the Liberal government and for expenditure on national defence, but his proposals were seen as a hostile campaign directed against the rich, and particularly the landowner. A measure which seemed to be more ominous for the landowner was his introduction of a 20 per cent tax on the unearned increment of land values, because in order to assess this it was necessary for government officials to undertake a comprehensive valuation of land, separating site value from

DUTIES ON LAND VALUES.

(Finance (1909-10) Act, 1910.)

REFERENCE: to be quoted in all correspondence.

Swaffry

32

RETURN TO BE MADE BY AN OWNER OF LAND OR BY ANY PERSON RECEIVING RENT IN RESPECT OF LAND.

(Penalty for failure to make a due Return, not exceeding £50.)

Reference to the accompanying Sheet of Instructions (Form 2—Land).

This space is not for the use of the person making the Return.

	Parish	*Swaffry*
	Number of Poor Rate ...	*1*
	Name of Occupier ...	*Hamond Thomas Astley Horace*
Particulars extracted from the Rate books	Description of Property...	*Brickfield*
	Situation of Property ...	*Bawsey*
	Estimated extent ...	Acres *26* Roods
	Gross Estimated Rental (or Gross Value in Valuation List*) ...	£ *35*
	Rateable Value	£ *29-15-0*

(* Applicable to the Metropolis only.)

IMPORTANT.—As the Land is to be valued as on 30th April, 1909, the particulars should be furnished, so far as possible, with reference to the circumstances existing on that date.

I. Particulars required by the Commissioners, which must be furnished so far as it is in the power of the person making the Return to give them.

(*a*) Parish or Parishes in which the Land is situated.	*Swaffry*
(*b*) Name of Occupier.	*The Owner*
(*c*) Christian Name and Surname and full postal address of the person making the Return.	*Thomas Astley Horace Hamond The Astley — Westacre Swaffham.*
(*d*) Nature of Interest of the person making the Return in the Land:—	*Life interest in*
(1) Whether Freehold, Copyhold, or Leasehold.	1 *Freehold*
(2) If Copyhold, name of the Manor.	2
(3) If Leasehold, (i.) term of lease and date of commencement (including, where the lease contains a covenant for renewal, the period for which the lease may be renewed), and (ii.) name and address of lessor or his successor in title.	3 (i.) 3 (ii.)

Form 4—Land.

WATERLOW BROS. & LAYTON, LIMITED, Printers and Stationers, 24 and 25, Birchin Lane, London, E.C. Works: Broken Wharf, Upper Thames Street, E.C.

Figure 21. First page of the infamous 'Form 4': The return concerning one 26-acre brickfield in which T.A.F.Hamond held a life interest.

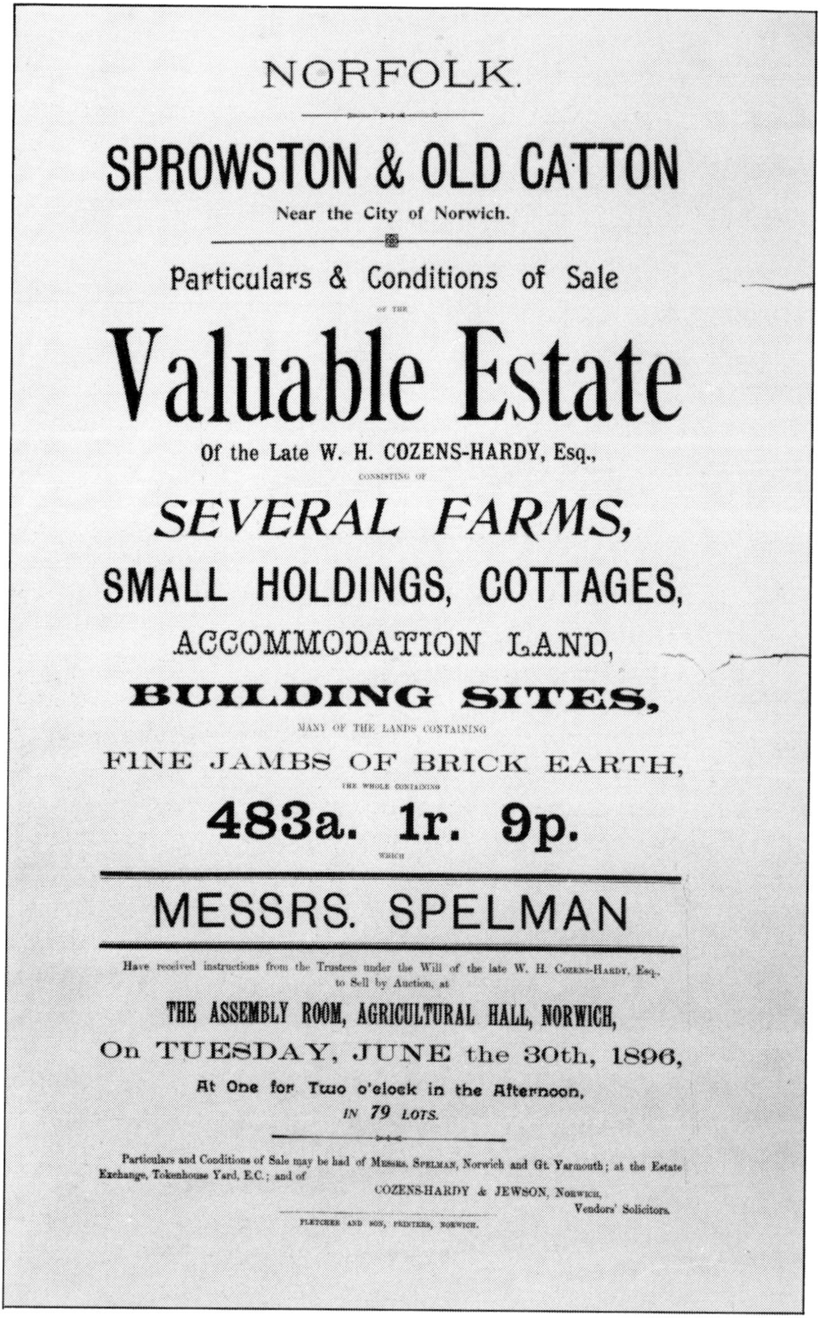

NORFOLK.

SPROWSTON & OLD CATTON

Near the City of Norwich.

Particulars & Conditions of Sale

of the

Valuable Estate

Of the Late W. H. COZENS-HARDY, Esq.,

CONSISTING OF

SEVERAL FARMS,

SMALL HOLDINGS, COTTAGES,

ACCOMMODATION LAND,

BUILDING SITES,

MANY OF THE LANDS CONTAINING

FINE JAMBS OF BRICK EARTH,

THE WHOLE CONTAINING

483a. 1r. 9p.

WHICH

MESSRS. SPELMAN

Have received instructions from the Trustees under the Will of the late W. H. COZENS-HARDY, Esq.,
to Sell by Auction, at

THE ASSEMBLY ROOM, AGRICULTURAL HALL, NORWICH,

On TUESDAY, JUNE the 30th, 1896,

At One for Two o'clock in the Afternoon,

IN 79 LOTS.

Particulars and Conditions of Sale may be had of Messrs. SPELMAN, Norwich and Gt. Yarmouth; at the Estate
Exchange, Tokenhouse Yard, E.C.; and of

COZENS-HARDY & JEWSON, NORWICH,

Vendors' Solicitors.

FLETCHER AND SON, PRINTERS, NORWICH.

Figure 22. Some landowners rationalised their estates. In 1896 the Cozens-Hardys of Letheringsett sold valuable landholdings near Norwich.

improvement, upon which a proper system of taxation might later be founded. In essence non-financial, it was seen as a deliberate provocation of, and attack against, the bastions of landownership. War against the landed interest had been declared.

Land Valuation Project

The Land Valuation project was a political gimmick which proved expensive to the tax-payer. It was mounted at a cost of more than £2 million but brought in a revenue of only one quarter of this. The Chief Valuer was paid a salary of £1,000-£1,200, and fourteen Superintending Valuers were appointed at salaries of £800-£850 a year. There were also forty-nine First Grade Valuers with annual salaries of £550-700, 107 Second Grade Valuers earning £350-£500, and three Technical Assistants on £150-250 per annum, as well as clerks and draughtsmen.

A major undertaking was imposed upon landowners in the completion of the necessary data required to assist the land valuers with their inquiry. The most controversial operation was the completion of 'Form 4', which 'enabled' a return to be made by the owner of land or by any person receiving rent in respect of land. The body of the form occupied four closely printed foolscap pages and there were two further pages of instructions. The whole thing was so complicated that the *Estates Gazette* surmised:

> Only the expert will be able to satisfy the Government requirements, and even he will find the task in some respects one of extraordinary difficulty.[2]

Completion of Form 4 involved such intricate detail and was so confusing that it seemed that most landowners would have to consult a solicitor or a surveyor, quite often both. On the 10,000 acre Westacre estate, for example, each of the ninety-five returns covered more than four pages! (See fig.21). Estate agents professed some surprise at the high valuations which came to be placed on estates by the government valuers. The Walsingham Abbey estate was valued by government valuers at £123,000. The agent wrote:

> I do not understand how these high figures have been arrived at

because to my mind an Estate that, after it has paid its mortgage interest, can barely pay its way cannot be worth so large a sum as is set down to it.[3]

A major portion of the estate changed hands in 1921 for the sum of £116,800, at prices pertaining during the postwar boom and considerably higher than they would have been before the war.

The Gaywood Hall estate was valued for death duty purposes at £28,000 in 1910, but the Inland Revenue questioned this valuation on the grounds that the Lloyd George Act of 1909-1910 affected its basis. They called for a revaluation of the whole Gaywood estate. The Valuation Officer maintained that, because Gaywood Hall was so near Kings Lynn, a considerable acreage was ripe for development and he therefore submitted a claim that the capital value was around £68,000, not the £28,840 returned under provisions of the 1894 Finance Act. This figure was eventually negotiated and agreed at £50,171. This revaluation raised the value of the estate from an eight per cent category into an eleven per cent category for the calculation of Estate Duty.[4]

Most landowners, however, had little reason to panic as far as the land valuation project was concerned, and this they quickly realised. In 1910 the *Estates Gazette* reassured its readers that the importance of the land valuation scheme was being over-emphasised by the government, and that it was a system which:

So far as our present needs are concerned, is as ludicrously over-adequate as would be the employment of a Nasmith steam-hammer to crack a filbert.[5]

In 1910, at the sale of the Didlington Hall estate, Howard Frank spoke of the political implications of the new system of land taxation. He assured his audience that not one acre of land on the Didlington estate would be subject to increased taxation.[6] Reporting on the state of the Norfolk land market during 1913, Stephen Gregory of Tilney wrote:

In my opinion the Finance (1909-1910) Act has not yet affected values. I do not think the so-called 'land campaign' has much disturbed us; it is generally regarded as the proverbial 'red herring'.[7]

Government valuers were inundated by the vast mass of material which began to find its way to Somerset House, and valuation proceeded painstakingly slowly. It was estimated that there would be perhaps ten million separate valuations. The *Estates Gazette* prophesied:

> It must be years before the end is reached, if ever it is. Meanwhile, the cost, direct and indirect, will be fabulous. ... The harvest, in fact, may not be ready for the reaping until it is too late to be of any value to the existing Administration.[8]

This proved to be correct. By 1915 the Undeveloped Land Duty and the Reversion Duty were already in abeyance, and it was obvious that the complete scheme for the valuation and taxation of the land would be abandoned. In 1920 Land Valuation Duties and the whole valuation system were abolished. Henry Asquith delivered the post mortem on the Land Valuation plans:

> They were crippled in their infancy, crippled and to a large extent mutilated in the Committee of this House. Still worse, after they had become part of the law of the land they were, if I can use the expression, disembowelled and to a great extent devitalised by the decisions of unsympathetic legal tribunals. Then at the critical moment came the war.[9]

The Land Campaign

In order to overcome the land taxers' frustrations at the delay in activating a vigorous land policy, Lloyd George decided on a big campaign 'to regenerate rural England'. He instituted a comprehensive investigation of the aspects of rural life which would need reform. An unofficial Land Enquiry Committee was appointed to provide information and recommendations which could form a basis of legislation. Writing to B.S. Rowntree he asked him 'to select a few parishes where the wages of the Agricultural Labourer are low and his housing bad but where the landlord lives in a fine house and keeps up a great style.' He suggested that Rowntree pick a few great houses from the pages of *Country Life* and then go and investigate the neighbourhood.[10] The success of the land campaign was immediately apparent in the villages, but the Liberals failed to stimulate the enthusiasm and support of the urban voter.

The Land Campaign was thrust aside when the war broke out in 1914, and after the war Lloyd George, now Prime Minister, was actively engaged in remodelling a new, postwar Britain, and so his ardour for land reform subsided. The metamorphosis of landholding was accomplished, not by land campaigns and the efforts of land reformers, but by voluntary unloading of landed estates on to the land market.

Lloyd George's campaigns were levelled primarily against the great landowners such as the Bedfords, the Buccleuchs, the Derbys, the Devonshires and the Northumberlands, whose land was valued in excess of £150,000 annually. In Norfolk only the Earl of Leicester could have been included within the ranks of the truly wealthy, and he was exceptional amongst the rich owners in that he relied principally upon farm rents for income. Extensive poverty in England was in direct contrast to the extreme riches of the great landowners and it was the very wealthy landlords whom Lloyd George wished to confront and to 'tax out of existence'. His gibe at Newcastle that 'a fully-equipped Duke costs as much to keep as two Dreadnoughts: and Dukes are just as great a terror and they last longer' illustrated not only his wit but also his determination to attack landed privilege. The irony of the situation is that, although it was the very great landowners who were the targets of the Liberal measures, they were the ones most able to withstand the assaults of Lloyd George. Attack was not levelled against the struggling squires *per se* but depression had so diminished the financial reserves of many of the smaller landowners that increased tax liabilities, especially death duties, were potentially crippling to them. Such owners had good cause for anxiety at a time of mild inflation and when it was difficult to raise rents to realistic levels.

The most significant reaction of landowners to the assaults of the land reformers was defensive. They wished to justify their position as landlords, not individually but as a class, and to refute allegations that they held a monopoly of wealth, or that they were idle or parasitical. Just because there was some truth in allegations against landlords, the need to refute vindictive statements seemed especially urgent. So long as claims against landlords were exaggerated, the best method of defence was exuberant counter-argument. Therefore landowners were at pains to demonstrate the unfairness of fiscal policy to justify their position against anti-landlord movements. Taxes were constantly referred to as burdens, either crushing, overwhelming, destructive or annihilating, and demands of the Treasury were described as pitiless and ruinous. There were vehement cries of injustice, but vociferous landowners were crying wolf. They were not, before the First World War, suffering the imposition of penal taxation, and the flimsy stick brandished by Lloyd George was not the hefty club it was portrayed to be. If Liberal legislation could topple the balance and force sales, then estate finances were surely so precarious that imminent sales were inevitable.

Death Duties

> The tax gatherer: Death is a small thing compared to him. Death removes one generation only to make way for another, but the tax gatherer prevents the other from ever coming in to its heritage.[11]

In 1894 Harcourt, as Chancellor of the Exchequer, introduced Estate Duty. The new duty was charged at rates graduated according to the net value of the whole property passing on death, whereas with other taxes assessment was based on the value of the actual benefit to the beneficiaries. It was of direct significance to landowners because, for the first time, agricultural land was specifically included in death duty assessment. In fact, the immediate revenue from the new duty was relatively insignificant - the highest rate was eight per cent, and that was paid only on those few estates valued at over £1 million. This ruled out most Norfolk estates, but nevertheless death duties did take their toll on some. The introduction of the new duties 'sealed the fate' of the Heacham estate, for example. By the mid 1890s, this 2,800 acre estate had already become over-burdened with debt, exacerbated by the effects of the agricultural depression. Declining agricultural income during the depression, together with family settlements and other obligations, had so undermined the position of the estate's finances that it became obvious to Eustace Rolfe, the owner of Heacham, that payment of the 1894 death duties would have been an intolerable burden for whoever succeeded to his estate. In letters to his daughter Amy, Eustace Rolfe wrote:

> The fact is that the new Succession duty laws will simply ruin the

estate if I left it to my brother or my nephews, charging it besides with what I consider your fair share of it.

Suppose I passed the property to Clive (his eldest nephew) - First he would pay Succession duty in the third degree which would mean that he must sell the Estate, and my own belongings would not get a decent income. If I left it to one of my brothers - Uncle Ernest or Uncle Charley - they are so nearly my age that duties would have to be paid twice in a few years.[12]

Eustace Rolfe sold his estate later that year.

Rates of taxation on the death of an estate owner continued to rise during the 1900s and had been more than doubled by the Liberal Governments by the outbreak of war in 1914. That year further tax increases were imposed, with rates being raised on estates over £1 million from eight per cent to twenty per cent. In 1919 they rose to forty per cent. To some people this five-fold increase in Estate Duty within a five year span seemed mercilessly severe.

On occasions, however, it was more convenient to cite fiscal measures as the reason for sales than to admit to insolvency resulting from extravagance or inefficient administration. And for political reasons much was made at the time of the penalising effects of death duties as a reason for sales. For instance, when the Calthorpe estate in Norfolk was sold in 1911, the vendors stressed the need to sell to provide funds for the payment of death duties upon the death the previous year of the sixth Lord Calthorpe. But at the same time the successors were spending a great deal of money, acquiring a fleet of Daimlers and adding an entire new wing to their home in Winchfield.[13] At the time of Lord Calthorpe's death, top rate Estate Duty was eight per cent.

Sales were often forced upon successors when an owner's death was quickly followed by that of his heir. On the Hunstanton Hall estate, for example, four deaths occurred within twenty-one years. Hamon LeStrange died in 1918 and was succeeded by his son, Roland, who died a year after his succession. His son, Charles Alfred, inherited and died unmarried in 1933, when he was succeeded by his brother who died in 1939, also unmarried. Each time, death duties were incurred. It is hardly surprising therefore to find the following sale announcement in 1949:

Mr LeStrange will be obliged to sell Hunstanton Hall and gardens. His family has been in unbroken ownership for very nearly 1,000 years. The break is due the impossible burden of taxation.

By contrast the Astley family had survived at Melton Constable because their succession troubles had occurred in the nineteenth century rather than during the more punitive twentieth. Sir Jacob Astley succeeded his father in 1859 but died childless twelve years later, when he was succeeded by his brother Delaval. Sir Delaval died a year later, and his successor, Sir Bernard, died unmarried three years afterwards.[14] Had these misfortunes occurred half a century later, the estate would undoubtedly have suffered severely at the hands of the tax man.

Where a minor inherited there was greater chance of continuation of an estate: in this event death duties would perhaps occur less frequently. On the Gunthorpe estate Edward Bowyer Sparke died in June 1910. His only son died from meningitis the following month, and the estate was inherited by his five-year old grandson. The estate survived almost intact until the latter's death, sixty-three years later.

Death duties have been described as 'a capital levy of great severity at uncertain intervals'. It is the unpredictability of their incidence which landowners have often found especially disturbing. Such duties, of course, are not peculiar to owners of land but death duties press with exceptional severity upon agricultural land. The economic returns from land are comparatively unremunerative, and to produce an income on a par with other forms of investment requires a much greater initial outlay. The stringency of death duty payments seriously affects agricultural efficiency. Owners who are heavily taxed, and sometimes financially embarrassed by a sharp succession of death duty payments, are often quite unable to contemplate the heavy outlay necessary to put their farm properties in good and tenantable repair. There is always the danger that the whole farming industry might be seriously prejudiced by the removal by death duties of capital otherwise needed for the equipment and development of the land. Estate Duty drained agricultural capital between 1922 and 1932 of more than £20 million. This capital was required for the development of the land and for investment in farms, especially necessary in conditions of agricultural depression.

In 1946, at a time when farming and land values were already in a state of flux, death duties on the larger estates rose to seventy-five per cent. Furthermore, new laws closed up some of the legislative loopholes that had enabled owners to reduce their tax burden. The untimely death of an owner now gave many desperate heirs no option but to sell considerable acreages of land, as well as paintings and other family artefacts, and even led in several cases to the absolute extinction of estates. The pace of demolition sales increased. Valuable paintings and possessions were sold and some of the nation's most prestigious art treasures went abroad. The Attlee government was sensitive less to the plight of beleaguered land owners than to the dispersal of national treasures and to the future of Britain's heritage. It decreed that the Treasury might be willing to 'aid owners' by accepting land, mansions and works of art in lieu of some part of death duty payment. Thus the Treasury received several of the nation's most esteemed country houses together with their splendid contents and sometimes some magnificent pictures. When Henry George, in the 1880s, had advocated confiscation of land and property and general redistribution of the assets of the rich for the benefit of the masses, the idea had seemed ludicrous. When the marxists called for common ownership of the means of production, of which land was the most important, the notion had seemed radical in the extreme. But the report of the agricultural committee of the Independent Labour Party, endorsed by its National Council for submission to the 1924 Annual Conference, had been ominous for landowners:

> A Socialist policy must provide for nationalisation of the land. The term of transfer from private to social ownership should be based on the principle that private gain must be subordinate to the common good.[15]

Much of the envisaged confiscation has in fact been achieved through fiscal measures introduced since the second War. How civilised are our British revolutions! They occur without bloodshed, without the public even being aware of them.

NOTES

1. Seaman, L.C.B., *Post Victorian Britain, 1902-1951* (1966), p.25.

2. *Estates Gazette*, 20 August 1910, p.325.

3. NRO, Lee Warner Papers, Box 24, no.5, 441 x 6.

4. NRO, Bradfer Lawrence Papers, BL 22, part 3.

5. *Estates Gazette*, 7 May 1910, p.775.

6. *Eastern Daily Press*, 30 November 1910.

7. *Estates Gazette*, 3 January 1914, p.26.

8. *Estates Gazette*, 20 August 1910, p.325.

9. *Ibid*, 24 April 1920, p.614: Report on discussion of the Budget Speech.

10. Gilbert, B.B., 'David Lloyd George. The Reform of the British Landholding and the Budget of 1914', *Historical Journal*, 21 January 1978, p.125, quoting letters of Lloyd George to Rowntree, 25 August 1913, Lloyd George Papers C/2/2/44.

11. *Eastern Daily Press*, 9 September 1936. Quoting a speech by Lord Hastings at a 'Festival of the Land'.

12. Berry, V., *The Rolfe Papers: Chronicle of a Norfolk Family, 1559-1908*, (1979), p.201.

13. Cannadine, D., *Lords and Landlords: The Aristocracy and the Towns, 1774-1967*, (1980), pp.160, 170.

14. Lord Hastings, *The Astleys of Melton Constable, 1236-1936*, (1936).

15. Annual Report by the President of the Central (later Country) Landowners Association at 17th A.G.M., June 24 1924.

Chapter Four
The Land Market

Demand for land

In periods when farming becomes increasingly remunerative, tenant farmers are able and willing to pay more for their farms. Competition to acquire more agricultural land then grows more intense and prices paid for land rise accordingly. Competition increases further when wealth attracted from outside interests begins to dominate the market. However, as a result of intense competition in the land market land prices get pushed to such an untenable level that returns on money invested in landowning are no longer commensurate with yields from other forms of investment, and prices level off and then began to decline. This cyclical pattern occurred during the nineteenth century when the successful manufacturer, industrialist or banker invested the fruits of his labours in agricultural land or a shooting estate. In the second half of the twentieth century, on the other hand, it was more likely to be institutional investors who sought safe and profitable outlet for their funds. In both the 1870s and the 1970s, prices rose to unrealistic levels and then fell sharply. It should be noted that in both centuries this reversal in land prices coincided with a period of general economic recession.

The late 1840s heralded in a thirty year period of prosperity in British agriculture, when both farmers and landowners did well, for the huge demand for British produced food, together with considerable sums invested, made farming profitable. Demand for land outstripped supply and so competition forced up land prices. This upturn in agricultural fortunes coincided with a period of general prosperity, with a boom in the City, favourable trading conditions generally, and considerable amounts of capital available for land investment. Britain by the 1850s had become 'The Workshop of the World'. Vast fortunes were being amassed from industry, commerce and trade, hence a large supply of money seeking a reliable outlet. For a variety of reasons it was prudent to invest money in land. To consign savings to the bank was regarded as somewhat risky, and the fallibility of banking was confirmed by the failure in 1866 of Overend, Gurney & Co, and, in Norwich, by the collapse of Harvey and Hudson's Crown Bank. Land, on the other hand, 'did not run away', could not be stolen or destroyed by fire, was not until 1894 subject to death duties, had the potential of capital gain and provided excellent security for future borrowing. In addition to the financial advantages, there was considerable social cachet and political advantage attached to land ownership, therefore newcomers sought both political influence and the seal of respectability by purchasing land. Landownership was thus both the cause and the manifestation of success.

Until the 1870s demand for land outstripped supply. Only a small proportion of land ever finds its way onto the market: the amount of land nowadays offered for sale in an average year, in the region of 450,000 acres per year, amounts to only about one or one-and-a-half per cent of the country's total agricultural land.[1] In Victorian times it is likely that an even smaller proportion came up for sale, for much of the land of the larger estates was entailed and held under strict settlement. Its supply was further decreased by the custom of primogeniture, which was strongly adhered to in Norfolk, and indeed remains unusually prevalent in the county to this day. Consequently, Victorian land hunters competed for land which rose steadily in price from an average of £35 an acre in 1863 to a nineteenth century peak in 1876 of £57 an acre. But with the onset in the 1870s of the 'Great Depression' this trend reversed dramatically. The drop in land prices was more pronounced than the former rate of increase. From the 1870s' peak, land in 1886 fetched only £28 an acre, and £20 in 1896. Not until the Second War did land prices approach the high values pertaining in the 1870s.'*

'*See Chart 2: Sale prices of agricultural land.
See also Chart 3: The 'Real' Price of Agricultural land.

Sales of outlying portions

With profits dwindling alarmingly, some owners would have been tempted to relieve themselves of the burdens of landownership by unloading their estates on to the market during the 1880s and 1890s, but at the low land prices pertaining they generally preferred to bide their time, unless the situation was desperate. There was, however, a convenient and painless way of raising capital, and this was by selling off outlying portions of their land. Estates had, in many cases, been built up by piecemeal purchase of separate land parcels of varying sizes, and often additional lands were acquired through marriage. The Rackheath estate, for example, included land in Rackheath, Stalham, Great Plumstead, Beeston St Andrew and Crostwick. The Burlingham estates were equally far-flung: When Henry Negus Burroughes died in 1872 he left, in addition to the home estate, land at Coltishall and at Gonvilles Hall at Browick (near Wymondham), sizeable farms at Raveningham and Gillingham and Alburgh, and marsh land at Acle, Wickhampton, Raveningham and Limpenhoe, amounting in all to 2,443 acres. Some estates, on the other hand, were compact units embracing several close-lying villages. Lynford estate was comprised of the whole of the parish of Lynford, plus the greater portion of West Tofts, Mundford and Cranwick and part of Colveston.

Even at the depth of the depression there remained some interest in land acquisition from farmers who were attracted by the low prices pertaining in Norfolk. After 1880, for instance, there was an incursion of Scotsmen and Northcountry men to Norfolk and Suffolk. Although the majority searched initially for rented land, many were able to buy their holdings when they came on the market, and a smaller proportion bought outright on arrival in East Anglia. Most took up grazing and milk production instead of the native corn and stock, at a time of constant expansion of the milk market. Tenant farmers also swelled the ranks of potential purchasers, often buying to avoid the risk of dispossession, for tenants had no security of tenure until 1913, nor rights to compensation for disturbance on the sale of their holding before 1910. There were few estates which did not sell some land during the depression years.

In addition to sales of land for agricultural purposes, those landowners fortunate enough to own land near the outskirts of towns found that excellent profits could be gleaned from relatively small land sales as building land became in short supply. Between 1871 and 1911 the population of

Norwich increased from 80,000 to 121,000, and building land in the vicinity of Norwich was therefore in demand. Ten per cent of the working population of Norwich was employed in the building trade during the housing boom of the 1890s, when there was development on the outskirts of Norwich in such areas as Heigham, Catton, Sprowston, Eaton and Thorpe. Some landowners were favourably placed to make a worthwhile capital gain. The Unthanks of Intwood sold land in Heigham, off the existing Unthank Road, in the 1880s. The land was divided into plots for artisan housing, strips in York Street about ninety-one feet long with frontages of twenty-three feet costing £63, or fifty-one feet which cost £139, while pieces of land in Cambridge Street had thirty foot frontages. The annual value of each dwelling had to be at least £9, and every building was to be faced at the front and part of the sides with white bricks and covered with good slate or tiles. The vendor was responsible for gravelling the street.[2] The Cozens-Hardy family of Letheringsett owned particularly valuable land only two miles from the centre of Norwich in Sprowston and Old Catton, having frontages on to three main roads and situated 'in one of the most populous suburbs'. This land was sold in 1896, following the death of William H. Cozens-Hardy the previous year, and much of it was bought for comparatively high density housing in terraces. 483 acres realised £16,745,[3] double the value of agricultural land (Fig.22). Building land further out of Norwich was sold to accommodate larger residences, such as 252 acres of the Staffords' Costessey estate, much of which possessed excellent potential for building development in the 'gentleman's residence' category.[4] This sale in 1902 brought in £5,260. R.L. Bagge was also fortunate in the siting of his estate at Gaywood, near Kings Lynn. In 1925 he sold half-acre plots for £167 each.

It was not only on the borders of towns where land was in demand for building purposes. Resorts on the east coast of Norfolk were becoming fashionable as watering places after the arrival of the railways - the Great Eastern in 1876 and the Midland and Great Northern ten years later. Towards the end of the nineteenth century building land was required in burgeoning resorts such as Sheringham, Overstrand and Cromer to develop hotels, private residences, villas and terraced houses. The fifth Baron Suffield saw an opportunity to put his estate on a sounder footing. In 1888 he sold a portion of his Gunton estate at Overstrand in a highly successful auction. Eighty-eight building plots were offered, all of which were sold at prices ranging from £10 to £110 per plot, an average of £320 an acre, which was substantially more than the land's agricultural value.

Few Norfolk landowners could benefit to the extent of Lord Walsingham, who could offer the lease of a site at the junction of London's Piccadilly and Green Park, covering an area of nearly 20,000 feet with frontages to Piccadilly, Arlington Street and Green Park. After spirited competition the site was let at a ground rent of £5,110 a year.[5] He also gambled heavily on converting Walsingham House in Piccadilly into a club and hotel, but this project was not financially successful and in 1902 there was a fifteen days' sale, in 4788 lots, of the contents of the house.[6]

Sales during the agricultural depression

For some owners, selling off comparatively small acreages was not enough to stave off insolvency. When Lynford Hall was sold in 1895 the auctioneers had been appointed by Mr Justice Sterling in the Court of Chancery, in the case of Bulkeley versus Stephens. At Hanworth, William Frederick Windham's wife 'contrived to obtain the whole of what was left of Windham's property. He made over to her, in return for a ludicrously small sum, the reversion of Hanworth and the other settled estates, in fact everything he possessed, them filed his petition in bankruptcy'.[7] After the death of John Hall Morse-Boycott his son, Frederick Augustus, sold Sennowe Park by order of the mortgagees.

With the price of land dropping to only £20 an acre in the mid-1890s, the low prices encouraged a steady, though sometimes sluggish, market for estates. This market was increasingly financed from the proceeds of industry and commerce, rather than from landed wealth. Until the middle years of the nineteenth century, purchase of the limited number of estates which did come on to the open market had usually been by existing landowners, in many cases owners of extensive holdings in other counties purchasing shooting estates in Norfolk. However, from the 1880s it was business men and bankers who saw the potential for capital growth and who began to stake appreciable claim to Norfolk soil. Woolmer White, of Timothy White & Taylor, bought 4,100 acres at Salle in 1888. Thomas Cook, grandson of the founder of the travel firm, acquired 5,200 acres at Sennowe ten years later. Following the lead of the Gurneys, the doyens of the county's bankers, financiers acquired Norfolk estates after 1880. William John Birkbeck bought 2,523 acres of the Stratton Strawless estate in 1900 and the remaining 500 acres in 1902. This historic estate had been continuously owned by the Marsham family since the reign of Edward I. And in 1900 Henry Barclay bought Hanworth Hall, together with 2,504 acres of the estate.

Although most of the estates on the market in the 1880s and 1890s were initially offered for auction, they invariably ended up being sold by private negotiation. No sales were effected through auction. The misapprehension that the land market was inactive in this period stems from reports in the *Estates Gazette* which were based on the outcome of sales effected through the medium of the London Auction Mart and other public sale rooms. Initially most estates had, in fact, been offered for auction. Often seemingly unrealistic reserve values were attached to them: this attracted publicity and was also a useful way of testing the market at a time of acute price fluctuation. Woolmer White's Salle Park, for instance, had been withdrawn at the London Mart in 1888 and sold immediately after the auction. Barclay's Hanworth Hall estate had been offered for auction in 1900 with 5,755 acres at a reserve price of £136,000 but as the bidding had reached only £116,000 the property had been withdrawn. Barclay bought the hall and half the land by private agreement in 1900 for £85,000.[8] There was another abortive auction when the Lynford Hall estate was put up in 1895: this estate of 7,718 acres was considered to have been worth £250,000, but no realistic bid was forthcoming and the estate was withdrawn, to be sold privately four years later to Mr Henry Campbell. The Angerstein's Weeting estate, not far from Lynford, also took four years to sell, having been consigned to auction in London in 1897, and sold eventually to T.S. Hall in 1901.

Of those Norfolk estates which were offered for sale during the late nineteenth century only three (Rackheath, Elmham and Letton Hall) failed to find a purchaser until after the First War, and another (Houghton) was permanently withdrawn. The Rackheath Hall estate was offered for sale by Sir Edward Stracey in 1895. The Buxton and Oxnead portions of the estate were described as 'some of the best land in the Eastern Counties' and Oxnead Hall, the remnants of the Pastons' great house, was of considerable historic interest. Nevertheless, the estate was withdrawn in 1895 and it was not until 1919 that it was finally sold.

The most important sale of the period was Houghton in 1886. This estate of 17,000 acres was owned by the Cholmondeleys, who lived at Cholmondeley Castle on their equally extensive Cheshire estates. In 1886 the *Eastern*

Daily Press described the Houghton estate as

> One of the most princely properties in the United Kingdom, embracing over 17,000 acres, the residence ... taking rank as one of the principal houses in Norfolk.[9]

But the market for 'princely properties' was at any time restricted, and particularly so in 1886, which probably accounts for the disappointing results at the auction. The bidding started at £230,000, and proceeded by bids of £10,000 up to £300,000, at which sum it was bought in. The Marquis of Cholmondeley kept his Norfolk estates and sold instead part of his more realisable Nantwich estate in Cheshire.

Elmham was also unsuccessful, both at auction and when offered privately. This was an excellent shooting estate of 4,772 acres belonging to Earl Sondes, who was also a considerable landowner in Kent. The auctioneer, Mr Oakley, was perhaps tired of abortive auction sales, for he suggested £100,000 as a suitable opening bid, and when he found himself faced with an unresponsive audience he withdrew the lot immediately with the remark that its reserve price was £125,000. Howard Frank conducted sales with greater panâche. He was a popular auctioneer from London and a regular at sales of Norfolk properties. At the auction of Lord Cranworth's Letton Hall estate in 1913 the opening bid was a mere £40,000. With good humour Mr Frank thanked the gentleman for this offer but made it clear he did not consider it a realistic bid. Even when put up in separate lots, the main lot failed to find a buyer, and consequently the greater part of the estate was withdrawn.

This technique of splitting up an estate into separate lots was a new practice in Norfolk, for until 1911 estates were auctioned as complete units. This method was completely superseded after 1911. The situation on the land market had altered, as greater agricultural prosperity had encouraged increasing demand for individual farms, and higher profits were obtainable from sales of smaller units. Changes in selling methods initiated progressive movement from London to the provinces, as local agents took over from London firms, conducting auctions at local sale rooms rather than at the London Mart in Tokenhouse Yard. It was still often practice to offer estates first as a whole, but if this met with an unsatisfactory response they were immediately offered in separate lots. If land was sold in smaller units it increased its appeal for local purchasers, who were usually farmers on the

Table 1: PARTICULARS OF ESTATE SALES, 1879-1940

Estate	Date	Acres	Venue	Agent
Wretham	1879	6556	London	Beadel & Co
Brooke House	1879	3110	London	Norton, Trist, Watney
Houghton	1886	17000	London	Clark & Co.
Sennowe	1887	4400	Norwich	Osborn & Mercer, London
Salle	1888	4100	London	
Riddlesworth	1893	4200	London	Beadel, Wood & Co.
Lynford Hall	1895	7718	London	Debenham, Tewson, Farmer & Bridgewater
Rackheath	1895	3000	London	Hampton & Sons
Elmham	1896	4767	London	Daniel, Smith & Oakley
Weeting	1897	7307	London	Beadel, Wood & Co.
Shadwell	1898	11444	Private	Beadel, Wood & Co.
Heacham	1899	2787	Private	
Westacre	1899	10139	Private	
Hanworth	1900	5756	London	Debenham, Tewson, Farmer & Bridgewater
Kilverstone	1900	4294	Private	
Stratton Strawless	1900	3007	Private	
Didlington	1910	5036	London	Knight, Frank & Rutley
Lexham	1911	2980	London	Trollope & Co.
Brooke Hall	1912	2980	Norwich	Hampton & Sons, London + Sewell & Brereton, Nch.
Letton	1913	4498	Dereham	Knight, Frank & Rutley
Weeting	1917	5930		Sold before auction
Bylaugh	1917	8150	Norwich	Irelands, Norwich + John Wood, London
Stratton Strawless	1918	3077	Norwich	Arnolds N'wich + Woodward Stowmarket
Costessey	1918	3136	Norwich	Norbury-Smith, London
Thursford	1919	1545	Norwich	Irelands
Burlingham	1919	5000	Norwich	Bidwells, Norwich + Daniel-Smith & Oakley
Gunton	1919	5879	Norwich	Irelands
Elmham	1919	2360	Norwich	Sewell & Brereton
Brooke House	1919	2333	Norwich	John Wood, London
Rackheath	1919	2683	Norwich	Spelmans
Taverham	1919	3104	Norwich	John Wood, London
Taverham	1920	3104	Norwich	Harry Arnold
Shotesham	1920	4633	Norwich	Grant, Stevenson & Co.
Shotesham	1921	2600	Norwich	do
Morley Hall	1921	2053	Norwich	Hall & Palmer, Wymondham
Thurning	1922	1550	Norwich	Mealing Mills, Norwich
Weston	1926	1913	Norwich	John Wood, London
Hockham	1930	3000	Watton	Knight, Frank & Rutley
Stanhoe	1932	500	Kings Lynn	
Honingham	1935	3265	Norwich	Hornors/Jackson, Stops
Gissing	1936	1274	Diss	Gaze
Necton	1940	2750	Private	Knight, Frank & Rutley

Figure 23. Howe Hall Farm, part of the Brooke Hall estate, sold in 1912 with 380 acres for £4,700.

Figure 24. Hall Farm, the home farm of the Stratton Strawless estate. Sold in 1918 with 195 acres for £3,700.

Figure 25. Upgate Green Farm, Shotesham all Saints, eventually sold in 1921 for £3,000.

Figure 26. The village of Mundford, with typical pairs of estate cottages on the left.

estate, or neighbouring landowners and businessmen. Local pre-sale publicity was more effective in stimulating interest from those people living within the area, since they were more likely to attend auctions held in their neighbourhood than to journey to London on the off-chance of acquiring comparatively small acreages. Strangers from outside the area could easily travel to the region if they were sufficiently interested.

'Stupendous Transactions'

From about 1910 owners began to sell their estates in response to growing demand for farms, and this trend reached a peak in the postwar boom. By the later stages of the First War there was at last a keen and seemingly inexhaustible demand for farms. Farming profits increased after 1906, and agriculture was extremely profitable during wartime, hence the strong revival in the land market from 1917 onwards. The beginning of a significant improvement in owners' ability to sell their estates was marked by the sale that year of the Bylaugh estate. At the end of the second day's sale of this 8,150 acre estate the auctioneer, Mr John Wood, announced that ninety per cent of the property had been sold. 5,106 acres were sold directly at auction, realising the sum of £93,615, and further property sold by private negotiation led to sale of all but twenty-one of the 140 lots offered. The successful outcome of the Bylaugh sale demonstrated not only the important improvement in the land market, but also the soundness of dividing estates into many lots, the multiplicity of the lotting being so novel that the Press reported it as a special feature of the sale. In the same year, 1917, the Weeting Hall estate of 5,930 acres was put on the market, and the estate was sold to Sir James Calder prior to the auction.

In 1918 sales increased in volume with a ready response from eager purchasers. Costessey Park was auctioned that year, when only four of the eleven farms were withdrawn and the remainder realised £260,000. A boom had arrived.

1919 witnessed an avalanche of Norfolk estate sales and broke all records for the number of sales successfully concluded and for the acreage which changed hands. At the Brooke House sale almost all of the 2,333 acres were sold. The same applied to the Tunstead estate, put on the market by T.H. Mack after the death of his father, when all the 1,135 acres which remained of the estate were sold at auction. The remaining 2,360 acres of the Elmham

Hall estate sold readily, with keen competition for the farmland, most of which sold for £29,812, although (not unusually in this period) there was no bid for the fine Georgian mansion with its well timbered park of 100 acres. Sir Edward Stracey sold 2,683 acres of his Rackheath estate to a land developer for £60,000, having retained the mansion and 600 acres. The Taverham Hall estate of 3,104 acres was sold at auction in one complete lot, again involving a land developer, who paid £52,000 for the estate.

It is not surprising, therefore, that there was a discernible note of awe in the *Estate Gazette*'s review of the market of 1919. In January 1920 the editor wrote:

> A more active and phenomenal year can scarcely be remembered in the real estate world than 1919, the total realisations of which have never been surpassed, being unprecedented and indeed breaking all records. With the continued breaking up of innumerable ancestral domains, all England seemed to be changing hands, every county being represented in the great revival and in the stupendous transactions.[10]

In no period before or since have so many estates been offered for sale or so great an acreage put on to the market, and at no time was completion of sale so easily accomplished. In the period 1917-1920 at least twelve of the 106 large estates in Norfolk were sold in their entirety, and very substantial portions of a further four also changed hands. In addition, an exceptional number of landowners took the opportunity to sell at least part of their estates. About one quarter of the acreage contained in the large estates in Norfolk changed hands within these three years.

This post-war boom changed the pattern of landownership. When estates were divided for sale, ownership was diffused among a greatly increased number of owners. Speculators bought intending to sell at a quick profit, private investors bought anticipating a further marked rise in land prices, local authorities bought to establish smallholdings. And land was acquired by the Forestry Commission who in 1918 were allocated the sum of £1.25 million from the Unemployment Fund with the object of promoting afforestation and relieving unemployment after the war. But the chief pressure of demand on the land market undoubtedly came from farmers. By 1917 wartime price increases had proved beneficial to them, and guaranteed prices under the Corn Production Act of 1917 brought further prosperity, especially in arable areas such as Norfolk. Tenant farmers had accumulated spare capital and felt confident in spending their wartime savings on farm purchase during the favourable postwar conditions. If their farms were sold over their heads, tenants lost their homes, and many of the farmhouses were delightful, some substantial properties. A further incentive for tenants to buy their holdings was the knowledge that rent increases were inevitable, because rents had been 'pegged' since 1917 and by the end of the war they were unrealistically low. The structure of landownership therefore underwent a rapid transformation.

This boom in the property market coincided with a postwar boom in the economy as a whole. Accumulated wartime savings were seeking an outlet and the full force of inflated money incomes was let loose on the economy. The sudden surge of demand forced up all prices, which had almost doubled anyway during four years of war. This was especially true in the housing market where shortages were most acute. Despite this price inflation, however, agricultural land was cheap in relation both to the general price index and to the rise in agricultural profits. Purchasers were there in abundance, hence the easy transfer of a quarter of the agricultural land of England and Wales, but with so much land on the market farm prices did not actually rise much higher than those reached before the war (Chart 2). Land prices rose from £22 an acre in 1907-11 to £33 in 1920, but in 'real' terms, allowing for inflation, this represented only one quarter of the peak prices of £57 in the 1870s[11] (See Chart 3). One can only assume from this that landowners took advantage of a sales outlet which had not been available to them for forty-five years, and that profit was less important a motive for selling than achieving relief from debts and the burdens of landownership.

Land Speculators and Property Companies

The decision facing many estate owners at the end of the First War was not whether to sell, nor when to sell, as much as **how** to sell. There were disadvantages attached to disposal of complete estates under the hammer. Firstly, the auction routine often involved protracted private follow-up negotiations to clear the portions which remained unsold after the auction. Secondly, and to many landowners a greater disincentive, the act of putting an estate up for auction could generate strong opposition from tenant farmers anxious about their livelihood. The Central Landowners' Association complained that the Farmers' Union was endeavouring to curtail

CHART 2: Sale Prices of Agricultural Land in England and Wales, 1870 - 1939

£ per acre

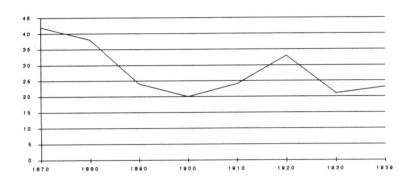

CHART 3: The "Real" Value of Agricultural Land in England and Wales, 1870 - 1950

$1870 = 100$

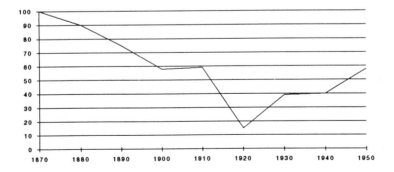

Source: J T Ward, Thesis op cit, Chart 20, p. 225.

owners' rights to sell freely to the highest bidder. The Union vigorously maintained that the occupying tenant had a claim to his farm which should not be subjected to outside competition if he wished to purchase his holding. In November 1919 two cases were heard before Mr Justice A.T. Lawrence in the Kings Bench Division, arising out of a disturbance at an auction in Brecon, caused by objection to an outsider bidding against the tenant of a farm. At Worcester in the same year 1919, tenants had invaded the sale room, mobbed the auctioneer, and stopped the sale.[12] Such heated exchanges between tenants and auctioneers were rare, but an owner undoubtedly faced unpopularity from tenant farmers when instructions were carried out to sell a complete estate outright through the medium of the public auction.

An alternative method of selling an estate was to offer the land at valuation to existing tenants, and then to unload the unsold portions by auction. However, this again was not entirely satisfactory from the point of view of either the tenant or the estate owner. In some cases the valuation was so high that the tenant paid more than the price realised at the succeeding auction. Tenants on the Gunton Hall estate, for example, in 1919 paid an average of £26 an acre for their holdings, while the remaining land was sold for only £19 an acre.[13] This was unusual, but during the postwar boom prices were so volatile that it became extremely difficult to gauge the value of land with accuracy. It was more likely that, in the gamble of estimating likely sale results, the landowner was himself in danger of losing heavily.

The landlord faced a dilemma. If he allowed his land to be auctioned he faced unpopularity and uncertainty. Alternatively, he might display a sense of responsibility to his tenants by choosing to give them the first option on the sale of their holdings at a reasonable valuation. But in many cases such fulfilment of old paternal obligations was delicately balanced against a pressing need to reorganise personal finances. Sometimes, indeed, owners were not free to exercise their discretion in facilitating land sales to tenants, for a limited owner was legally bound to obtain the best price for his land when contingent interests, as well as his own, were at stake.

There was, however, one way of selling entire estates which relieved owners of both the tedium of individual private negotiations and the rigours of the auction procedure, and that was to sell outright to land speculators and property companies. Direct sale to a land speculator in this manner was a business transaction which relieved landowners from the wrangles and complications otherwise involved in estate sales. To a syndicate of speculators the profit motive was sufficiently forceful to overcome inhibitions over long-standing obligations and the hostility of tenants. There was considerable activity on the part of syndicates who bought estates 'en bloc' in order to sell in lots, particularly during periods of strong demand for farms between 1905 and 1922. Middlemen's profits were said to have amounted to £250,000 in the County of Lincolnshire alone on the turnover there of 50,000 acres.[14]

One such speculator active in Norfolk was Walter Abel Towler, a farmer from Littleport in Cambridgeshire. In May, 1924, he bought the 7,713 acre Lynford Hall estate from J.O. Montagu. In the following September he sold 6,208 acres to the Forestry Commission, and three months later he sold the remaining 1,505 acres and Lynford Hall to the Country Breeding Estates Company Ltd. This was not Towler's first foray into Norfolk property: On 28th July, 1917, he had purchased the Bylaugh Park estate of 8,155 acres from Major E.H. Evans-Lombe at an agreed price of £120,000. On 11th August, 1917, he sold out to A. Wilkinson and J.W. Newcombe of the Newcombe Estates Company Ltd for the sum of £127,000.[15] Towler therefore made a clear profit of £7,000 within a fortnight on just one successful transaction. Evans-Lombe had benefitted also by selling his estate to a speculator in that he was saved the disturbance and possible unpopularity of a public auction instigated by himself as landowner, while being guaranteed immediate sale of the complete estate without various lots being left unsold. The Newcombe Estates Company quickly regained most of the money they had expended, for they divided the 8,155 acre estate into lots for auction within six weeks of purchase. On September 28/29 1917, 5,105 acres were sold directly at auction,[16] realising the sum of £93,615.[17] Other lots were sold by private treaty, the Hall in its park of 736 acres being purchased in 1918 by the Marsh family of Warwick.

The Newcombe Estates Company Ltd was incorporated with a nominal capital of £50,000 in December 1905. Originally the activities of the Company were confined to the Market Harborough and Birmingham area, but from 1909 they gradually extended their catchment area to Weston Super Mare, Southampton, Southsea, London, etc., concentrating until the First War mainly on small residential developments. Their Norfolk activities included, in addition to Bylaugh, the Stratton Strawless estate of 3,077 acres from W.J. Birkbeck's executors in March 1918. This estate they resold in May 1918.[18]

Speculative buying was at a peak during the postwar years, for during the boom years from 1917 to 1921 demand for farms in Norfolk was such that a quick turnover of land was likely and easy profits could be made. Prior to the First War this was not the case, for in the 1905-15 period the land market fluctuated considerably and speculators' capital might be tied up for long periods before showing a profitable return. For instance, in February 1911 Earl Sondes sold a large acreage from his Elmham Hall estate to F.J. Huckleby, who put 1,933 acres up for auction the following August.[19] This coincided with a marked decline in the land market, and at the auction many of the lots offered were withdrawn, and the only substantial lot sold was the 186 acre Silverstone Farm at North Elmham. The contract between F.J. Huckleby and Earl Sondes was rescinded, presumably because the result of the auction was so disappointing that the speculator had not the means to honour the contract. Lord Sondes seems not to have been unduly discouraged by his venture into business with a speculator, for the 1919 sale of 2,360 acres of the estate was also a speculator's sale, the vendor being Frederick W. Wateridge. This time most of the land was sold, either at the sale or immediately afterwards, and total sales realised £29,812.[20] However, if credence can be given to a hand-written note on the sale catalogue, the speculator was not making any immediate profit on his £29,812, for the cryptic message stated:

The price said to have been paid to Earl Sondes for the 2,360 acres now to be sold is £37,000.[21]

Frederick William Wateridge would have to wait in the hope of making a profitable return when the Hall and park of about 101 acres was sold. It is obvious that not all land speculators were reaping rich rewards.

During the years of the postwar boom, however, speculators had little difficulty in disposing of the estates they acquired. George Grant Stevenson bought and resold the Rackheath Hall estate successfully in 1919. There was brisk competition for the land on offer and only two farms remained unsold. Maybe this happy outcome compensated Stevenson for his disappointment over the Walsingham Abbey estate, for which he negotiated concurrently with Rackheath. In March 1919 he offered £120,000 for 5,152 acres and paid a deposit of £5,000. But he was gazumped and his contract rescinded by summons.[22] Another auction successfully accomplished by a middleman was of Costessey Hall estate in 1918, after Lord Stafford had sold his 3,000 acres to Herbert David Boret (or Borst). John Digby Mills sold the Taverham Hall estate of 3,000 acres by public auction in one complete unit in November

1919 to Lawrence B. Lister, who divided it for resale by auction in February 1920. Only two of the principal farms offered remained unsold, and the mansion was withdrawn but sold later to Revd F.W. Glass for use as a preparatory school.

During the 1930s land sales were not easily accomplished. But at least two estates were sold through speculators during this difficult decade. Percy Rampton, of Surbiton, Surrey, purchased the Hockham Hall estate from Henry Partridge, selling the Hall and 1,096 acres in September 1930, and a further 2,025 acres in November to the Forestry Commission. Albert Becheley-Crundal had more difficulty after paying £40,000 for the 4,323 acre Honingham Hall estate from the mortgagees of the second Lord Ailwyn, in 1935. Although there was a temporary improvement in market conditions at the time, three of the farms, having an aggregate reserve value of £6,000, remained unsold at auction. The hall was withdrawn at £5,000, the reserve being £10,000, but this, with the park of 161 acres, was bought in August 1936 by Sir Eric Teichman.

Middlemen performed a useful function in relieving landowners of the aggravation of selling their estates, to the mutual advantage of both parties. They aimed to make a quick and substantial profit from their activities, but there was an element of risk involved, and they were not cornering the market sufficiently to affect prices. Nevertheless, their actions aroused hostility because farmers were convinced that speculative profits inflated land prices. The antipathy aroused by the speculators is reflected in the following letter from the County Secretary of the National Farmers' Union, published in 1919:

The County Executive Committee of the National Farmers' Union desires to point out to the farmers of England the very serious position in which they are now being placed through the sale of landed estates to gambling syndicates. No tenant, great or small, will be safe so long as this system is allowed freedom to work its evil course, and if not checked will bleed agriculture white and destroy its vitality. This committee is convinced that this system may be arrested by all farmers refraining from bidding for any land that is offered for re-sale by syndicates.[23]

Missed markets

The 'stupendous transactions' and the phase of 'phenomenal' activity in the land market continued until the Autumn of 1920, after which the economy declined and the property market slumped. In February 1921 a discerning letter from George Lee Warner in Australia reached the trustees of the Walsingham Abbey estate, urging haste in the sale of the estate, to which he was heir:

Delay means loss of sale while the selling is good and will be fatal. The opportunity will not occur again possibly in our lifetime. *Press the sale* to Eustace Gurney *now* before it is too late, for the chance is slipping away.[24]

The sale of the estate was completed three months later, after four years of vacillation and procrastination. An offer of £120,000 had been made in 1919 by a Mr Stevenson and a deposit of £5,000 accepted, but the family preferred to sell to Sir Eustace Gurney, who was married to a relative, and seemed anxious to acquire the estate. Mr Stevenson applied to the Courts for confirmation of sale, but the contract was eventually rescinded, and Gurney bought the estate of 5,125 acres for £116,800 in May, 1921.[25]

However, not all landowners had Lee Warner's foresight and from mid-1920 activity on the land market in Norfolk became increasingly sluggish. Land prices fell very quickly. Much land was withdrawn from auctions or sold below the reserves at which it would have been bought in early 1920. 4,638 acres of the 7,759 acre Shotesham estate had been sold to a land speculator who put it up for auction in June 1920 when less than half of the land offered found purchasers, realising £42,000. A further auction of property which remained unsold was held in 1921, but there was again some lack of interest on the part of prospective purchasers. Prices, in fact, tended to be lower than those of the previous auction. For example, Upgate Green Farm, with house and 241 acres, had been bought in at the 1920 sale at £3,350, and in 1921 sold for £3,000.[26] This is good land, and such an outcome would have been most unlikely at the height of the boom. J.C. Crossley missed the market in July 1921 for the auction of his Morley Hall estate. When its 2,053 acres were offered for sale only Burfield Farm was sold. The Thurning Hall estate was put on the market in 1922 after the death in 1920 of James Gay, but this sale also was unsuccessful. Pickenham Hall

76

Figure 27. The south front of Lynford Hall, built 1856-61 to the designs of William Burn. The house costing £145,000 was sold by order of the mortgagees in 1895.

Figure 28. Rackheath Hall, 1919. Sir Edward Stracey retained the hall and surrounding woodlands when the estate was sold in 1919 to a speculator.

Figure 29. Ketteringham Hall, rebuilt by Sir John Boileau in the 1840s, and sold by his descendents to the trustees of the Duke of Westminster in 1947.

Figure 30. Kimberley Hall, the great Norfolk home of the Wodehouses, built to the designs of Talman and Prouse, sold in 1958.

estate of 5,000 acres was offered unsuccessfully in 1923, and put up for auction in 1924 when it was bought in at £65,000.[27] It was not until 1925 that the estate was finally sold, by private treaty to Mr J.S. Moreton. Although this was marginal land, there is no doubt that it would have sold more readily six years earlier.

In many cases legal restraints enforced delay. Much of the land had been entailed and was held under strict settlement, a legal device to safeguard the future of family estates against recklessness or ineptitude by limiting freedom to sell or to mortgage the land. More flexibility had been introduced as a result of Lord Cairns' Settled Land Act of 1882, which allowed a limited owner to sell, improve or lease his estate as though he were an owner in fee simple, almost the only fetter being restraint on selling the family mansion or heirlooms. Nevertheless, still many complications existed until the 1925 Act of Lord Birkenhead, and there remained estates which were not available for sale during the land boom after the First World War. In other cases owners missed the market through sheer procrastination. But whatever the factors involved - indecision, legal obstacles, or merely the inability of heirs to assume control of estates - many estates which might have been broken up or reduced in size were retained with their acreages intact.

The interwar period was a difficult time for farmers and landowners alike. As there was so little demand for farms, estates were more likely to be offered for sale in complete units once again, a reversion to the pre-1911 practice. Stanhoe was auctioned as a complete unit in 1932, but no bid was forthcoming. When offered next in thirty-seven lots, most were withdrawn. In the wake of many earlier sales of outlying portions, estates by this time were generally much reduced in size. Where a sale was accomplished it was often only after lengthy negotiation, with prices up to one third lower than those of a decade earlier.

Estate agents tried to interest purchasers by representing land as an investment offering safe security. 'Put your money where you can see it' was the maxim. This concept was especially reassuring during the recession of 1929-32, when the stock market was seriously disturbed. The *Estates Gazette* suggested in January 1934 that

Real property offers a better return than can be obtained from paper securities with greater safety than that afforded by any but high-priced investments.... The capital value of cultivable land is certain to rise materially above its present level.[28]

This prediction was a safe bet! In 1934-5 the outlook for agriculture seemed more optimistic, and the return on land investment was at least preferable to that on government stock. Farming did indeed improve a little in some areas during this period, stimulated by subsidies, protection and a buoyant home market. The Honingham estate was put up in 1935 during this marked, though temporary, improvement in market conditions. It took six hours to dispose of the 4,323 acres, offered in seventy-seven lots. Several lots did not secure sufficiently high bids to reach the reserves and were withdrawn, but nevertheless sales were effected to a total value of £41,660. In a continuing effort by land agents to boost sales potential customers were exhorted to 'take advantage of present market conditions to secure land to show you a generous yield with a certain prospect of capital appreciation and increasing security in the future.' Perhaps shrewd businessmen were not reading the *Estates Gazette* for there were no signs of their rushing to acquire land, or certainly not in Norfolk, anyway. After the Honingham sale the few estates which were placed on the market sold, if at all, with difficulty and often after protracted efforts. The value of farming land had reached a low point. Land had become a drug on the market, especially on the poorer soils which had almost no value at all in the 1930s. In 1938 11,500 acres of the Merton estate, including thirty farms and 200 houses, were valued for mortgage purposes at £87,000 - under £8 an acre. John Woods, when making his valuation, recommended a maximum mortgage of £50,000, or just over £4 an acre.[29]

There was further faltering of the market with the prospect of another war and signs of returning depression, and with the outbreak of war in 1939 land transactions were temporarily in abeyance.

The 1940s

During the Second War the Ministry of Defence acquired land in Norfolk, either for the duration of the war or under compulsory purchase. Land was taken over for airfields and for the Stanford battle area. As early as 1938 the Royal Air Force was flying Harrow aircraft from Feltwell, and Harrows and Hendons from Marham. There was a gradual build up of airfields by Bomber Command during the war. When America entered the war a massive construction programme was launched in Norfolk and Suffolk to provide airfields for vast formations of Fortresses and Liberator bombers of the United States Eighth Air Force, and more land was acquired for this purpose.

Figure 31. The sixth Lord Walsingham (1843-1919), described by the *Eastern Daily Press* in 1919 as 'perhaps the most versatile man in the peerage'.

Figure 32. Spy's cartoon of the second Earl of Leicester (1822-1909) from *Vanity Fair*, 1883.

The Ministry of Defence compulsorily purchased 1,000 acres of the Pynkney estate to build Sculthorpe Airfield. In 1940 an area of 118,000 acres of marginal land near Thetford was obtained by the War Office under Defence Regulation 52 to form the Stanford battle area. The inhabitants of Tottington, Sturston, Stanford, Langford and most of West Tofts were given one month's notice to leave their homes. After the war the bulk of the land was de-requisitioned but the camps at Bodney, East Wretham and West Tofts were retained to a total acreage of 27,000 acres, reduced later to 17,700 acres. This land had been purchased from the Clermont, Lynford Hall and Wretham estates, but mostly leased from the Merton estate at 1940 rent levels, then compulsorily purchased in 1950.

Farm incomes doubled during the war, for farming was well supported by the government. Throughout the 1940s land prices increased, especially after the war when they rose from £45 an acre in 1945 to £76 by 1949. The nominal price of land had returned to that of eighty years earlier, although in 'real' terms land was now worth about half the 1870s price, as Chart 3 illustrates.

In the aftermath of the second war landowners were hit not only by general economic recession but also by the then radical policies of the new Attlee government. In spite of farmers' prosperity, net rental incomes rose much less than inflation, for restrictions on rents, imposed during the war, were continued. With death duties on the larger estates now up to a punitive seventy-five per cent, there was an ever-increasing weariness with the struggle to withstand financial pressure in a changing world in which the prospects for landownership seemed unrewarding. Many estates had already been reduced to ownership of only the hall and park and a few farms, and in a spate of land sales and demolition of country houses, the landowners continued to cast off their lands and quit their decaying, unmanageable houses. Riddlesworth Hall was sold in 1946 and became a school; in 1948 Mrs Rosemary James sold the family home at Garboldisham Old Hall; and in 1949 the last sixty-four acres of Stanhoe were sold to a Wisbech fruit farmer. Ketteringham Hall estate was sold to the Trustees of the Duke of Westminster in 1947. Sir Lawrence Jones, who had sold most of the Cranmer Hall estate during the 1930s to the sitting tenants, sold the remaining 394 acres in 1946. He commented that taxation had reached such a height that he could not hope to earn enough in the City to keep going a country home of the size of Cranmer. It had become difficult to engage servants, and he calculated that it needed an invested capital sum of £10,000 to maintain a single gardener. 'The end of an age had arrived, an age of leisure and pleasure, and of living on the backs of men and women who were no longer of a mind to bear our weight.' A public auction attracted not a single bidder, and in the end Cranmer was sold 'for a song' to a farmer who eventually removed the top floor, made three houses out of one, and finally pulled half of it down.

For a time fowls scratched and moulted where there had been green lawns, and then gave place to a wilderness.[30]

The years of revival

The despondency continued during the 1950s, when more estates were broken up or sold. In 1951 the Oxburgh Hall estate, the home since 1482 of the Bedingfields, was sold with its 3,563 acres to the Ashdale Land and Property Company of London, who put it up for public auction later in the year. Many of the properties were sold to the tenants by private treaty prior to the sale, but Oxburgh Hall itself was bought back by Lady Sybil Bedingfield, Sir Edmund's mother, with the aid of the Pilgrim and Dulverton Trusts and the Gordon Daviot Fund.[31] In October 1952 she presented it to the National Trust, saving it from the threat of demolition. Dunston Hall estate was sold in 1957 by private treaty. The family had lived there for 300 years.[32] Congham Hall had been burnt down in 1939, and the Elwes family sold the estate in 1956. The Hardley and Thurton sections of the Langley Park estate were sold in 1954, and the remainder of the estate in January 1957 to Broadland Properties Ltd, who resold the following June. Most of the Kimberley Hall estate was sold to a syndicate for almost £250,000 in July 1958,[33] and the following October the bulk of the remaining portions was sold for about £47,000. Kimberley Hall itself, the garden house, the park land and the home farm, about 632 acres in all, were later resold by private treaty for about £40,000.[34] In 1958 the Quidenham Hall estate of 3,500 acres was sold to the Eagle Star Insurance Company, the hall having been owned since 1948 by Carmelite nuns.

Although the sales carried on apace into the late 1950s, by the end of this decade the prospects for landownership were improving. The Conservative government reduced levels of taxation and issued building licences. The gloom dispersed and confidence began to return. Land prices rose slowly, from £76 an acre in 1949 to £101 in 1959. Country houses were restored, redecorated and re-equipped with modernised central heating and up-to-date plumbing systems. Others were entirely rebuilt, as on the Woodrising estate where, in 1958, Lord Verulam received planning approval for a new hall to replace the old one which had lain deserted after being requisitioned during the war.

Many landowners were farming a considerable acreage of their land on their own account, thus benefitting, at the time, from considerable tax concessions. In-hand farming also had the advantage in times of inflation of mitigating the effects of the rent lag. But by the late 1950s rents, always slow to respond to changing circumstances, were at last adjusting to a more realistic level. This inflexibility of rent movements had benefitted landowners at the onset of the 1870s depression, but it took fifteen years after the ending of the Second World War before rents adjusted sufficiently for the landlords to share with farmers the benefits of the recovery in agriculture.

NOTES

1. Report of the Committee of Inquiry into the Acquisition and Occupancy of Agricultural Land (Northfield Report), Cmnd 7599, 1977, p 67.

2. NRO, Access Correspondence from Miss Unthank, 'Heigham Sale of Building Plots', October 1971.

3. Spelmans' Sale Catalogue, 1896.

4. NRO MC/18.

5. *Estates Gazette*, 31 July 1886, p 369.

6. NRO Walsingham Manuscript 21554 XVlll/23.

7. Ketton Cremer, R.W. *Felbrigg: the story of a house* (1962), p 264.

8. NRO MC 19/152 444 x 8/9: Letter from Edward Tewson to Messrs Steele, 21 College Hill, London, 23 July 1900.

9. *Eastern Daily Press*, 23 July 1886.

10. *Estates Gazette*, 3 January 1920, p.12.

11. Ward, J.T., 'A Study of Capital and Rental Values of Agricultural Land in England and Wales between 1858 and 1958', PhD Thesis, London (1960),pp 225,273.

12. *Estates Gazette*, 20 September 1919, p.377.

13. *Ibid*, 27 December 1919, p.883.

14. *The Times*, 17 and 19 May 1919.

15. NRO EVL 33 446 x 6, 1917: Agreement for the sale of the Bylaugh Park Estate including plan. With agreement for sub-sale by Towler to Albert Wilkinson in 1917.

16. *Eastern Daily Press*, 29 September 1917, and 1 October 1917.

17. *Estates Gazette*, 5 January 1918, p.10.

18. NRO MC 14/95, 388 x 67.

19. NRO MC 14/27, Elmham Sale Catalogue, 388 x 6/7.

20. Year Book of Auction Sales, 1911 (Published by the Estates Gazette Ltd, London).

21. C & R, C658.844 ELM, Sale Catalogue 1919 Elmham Estate.

22. NRO Lee Warner Papers, Box 6: Account of my Trusteeship, Letters etc 1908-1948.

23. *Eastern Daily Press*, 9 June 1919, Letter of J F Wright, County Secretary of the National Farmers' Union, Aldeby.

24. NRO Lee Warner Papers, Box 6, Letter from George Lee Warner to trustee Alfred Lee Warner, 27 February 1921.

25. *Ibid*, Box 6, Accounts, 15 July 1921.

26. NRO MC 14/113, also C & R, Q C658.844 for 1920 Sale. NRO MC 14.117 for 1921 sale.

27. *Estates Gazette*, 5 May 1923 p 643 and 10 May 1924, p 629. Also Year Book of Auctions 1924.

28. *Ibid*, 6 January 1934.

29. Information kindly given by Lord Walsingham.

30. Jones, L.E., *Georgian Afternoon* (1958) p 249.

31. *Eastern Daily Press*, 4 October 1951.

32. *Ibid*, 16 May 1957, 13 July 1957.

33. *Ibid*, 21 July 1958, also C 658.844 KIM, MC 39/407 487x6.

34. *Ibid*, 17 October 1958.

Conclusion

This book has traced the influences which determined the behaviour of Norfolk landowners through eighty long, unprofitable years, from the early years of agricultural depression in the 1870s and the low controlled rents of the First World War, through the tribulations of the interwar period, to an upturn in prosperity during the late 1950s. A considerable decline in the preeminence of landed estates has been noted, and the evidence gives every indication that the position of the landowner in the rural scene has diminished perceptibly and constantly since the end of the First World War. The decline has been especially pronounced amongst the minor gentry and the squires, who were too vulnerable to economic misfortune to withstand a long period of income decline. Very few of these smaller estates survived in the ownership of their original families.

The wealthier landowners were better able to contend with depression. Eight of the eleven great estates (over 10,000 acres) in Norfolk were still thriving in 1983 in the hands of the same families cited by Bateman one hundred years earlier. Of the fifty-six estates in the 3,000 to 10,000 acre range, eighteen of the original fifty-six remained with their original families. Many were much reduced in size, but all retained at least 1,000 acres (suggested by the Country Landowners' Association as the dividing line between farm and estate). These larger owners had the advantage of size, being able to sell part of the estate and so raise money to support the remainder. Very often, on estates of all sizes, continuation of ownership was ensured only by the bolstering of estate finances with an additional income from non-agricultural sources.

After the First World War the impression was given that 'all England seemed to be changing hands', and in each succeeding decade the demise of the landowner has been remarked upon. But the landowners have proved remarkably tenacious in retaining estates in spite of political obstacles, economic setbacks and rising costs of administration. Reduction of acreage is not entirely synonymous with decline: a landlord with 1,000 acres is still in receipt of a substantial gross income, and estate profits are often further increased by in-hand farming.

There is a time lag between changes in farming profits and movements of rent levels. We found that, in the 1870s, it was tenants who bore the brunt of the impact of the depression because landlords were slow to make effective reductions in contractual rents. When farming profits recovered temporarily in the first two decades of the twentieth century landowners did not raise rents to an economic level, and therefore suffered a decline in income which was exacerbated by wartime rent controls. And the 'bleak years' for landowners lasted fifteen years longer than the interwar depression.

The general public today tends to tolerate the existence of a landed nobility as a relic of the Victorian era, equating the landowner with the penniless earl exhibiting his stately home to visitors whose admission fees and selected sales of contents assist in keeping a roof over his head. The image is well-preserved, supported by accounts of the ravages of taxation and the crippling cost of maintenance of ancestral homes. But the landowner is, in fact, a businessman. The garnering of rewards from landownership calls for great expertise, business acumen and capital investment in agriculture. There is constant pressure to innovate, to expand, and to substitute capital for labour. Farm incomes are largely linked to agricultural support prices. Problems of the European Economic Community create some apprehension as to the continuing prosperity of agriculture.

Rents fell in the closing years of the 1980s. The capital value of land and the income therefrom have dropped in the last few years. Farming needs support. In terms of the value of its output agriculture is the biggest industry in the United Kingdom. Landownership can only be profitable if farming is allowed to thrive.

Owners of Estates in Norfolk of 2,000+ acres in 1883

LANDED ARISTOCRACY: landowners with more than 10,000 acres

Landowner	Estate	Acres
Cholmondeley	Houghton	16,995
Hamond	Westacre	10,139
Hare	Stow Bardolph	11,310
Hastings	Melton Constable	12,737
Kimberley	Kimberley	10,805
Leicester	Holkham	44,090
Lombe, Evans-	Bylaugh	13,832
Orford	Wolterton	12,341
Suffield	Gunton	11,828
Townshend	Raynham	18,343
Walsingham	Merton	12,120

GREATER GENTRY: landowners with 3,000-10,000 acres

Landowner	Estate	Acres
Albemarle	Quidenham	7,340
Amherst	Didlington	9,488
Angerstein	Weeting	7,235
Applethwaite	Pickenham	5,135
Bagge	Stradsett	3,769
Bayning	Honingham	4,323
Beauchamp	Langley	6,768
Bedingfield	Oxburgh	4,800
Berney	Morton/Hockering	5,429
Berney	Barton Bendish	3,148
Birch	Wretham	6,556
Boileau	Ketteringham	3,626
Boycott	Sennowe	5,257
Buckworth	Cockley Cley	3,614

Bulwer	Heydon/Quebec	8,943
Burroughes	Burlingham	7,414
Buxton	Shadwell Park	9,309
Canterbury	Brooke House +	
	Great Witchingham	5,177
Chadd, Scott-	Thursford + Pynkney	6,242
Davy	Kilverstone	4,294
Elwes	Congham	3,313
Fellowes	Haveringland	4,083
Fellowes	Shotesham	7,778
ffolkes	Hillington	8,111
Fielden	Beachamwell	4,341
Fountaine	Narford	6,318
Gurdon	Letton	4,842
Gurney	Keswick, etc	8,498
Hare	Docking	3,778
Howard	Castle Rising	4,044
Jodrell	Salle	4,100
Jones	Cranmer	3,627
Ketton	Felbrigg	4,442
Le Strange	Hunstanton	7,802
Long	Dunston	3,555
Lothian	Blickling	8,073
Mackenzie	Croxton Park	5,700
Mason	Necton	4,050
Micklethwaite	Taverham	5,356
Mills	Clermont + Hilborough	8,000
Mott	Barningham	5,331
Newcombe	Feltwell	5,034
Norfolk,Duke of	Kenninghall	4,460
Nugent	West Harling	4,350
Pratt	Ryston	3,518
Preston	Beeston Hall	4,800
Sondes	Elmham	4,939
Sparke	Gunthorpe	3,775
Stephens, Lyne-	Lynford Hall	6,878
Stracey	Rackheath	4,842
Trafford	Wroxham	5,624
Upcher	Sheringham Hall	3,748
Wales, Prince of	Sandringham	8,079
Warner, Lee-	Walsingham Abbey	8,213

Weyland	Woodrising	4,098
Windham	Hanworth	6,483

LESSER GENTRY/SQUIREARCHY: Landowners with 2,000-2,999 acres

Landowner	*Estate*	*Acres*
Bagge	Gaywood	2,891
Bentinck	Terrington	2,802
Browne, Graver-	Morley Hall	2,053
Calthrop	Stanhoe	2,033
Cator	Woodbastwick	2,463
Custance	Weston	2,913
Durrant	Scottow	2,835
Gay	Thurning	2,282
Green	Ken Hill	3,000
Gurney	Sprowston Hall	2,594
Hardy, Cozens-	Letheringsett	2,929
Hemsworth	Shropham	2,868
Holmes	Brooke Hall	2,932
Irby	Boyland	2,460
Jodrell	Bayfield	2,407
Kemp	Gissing	2,133
Keppel	Lexham	2,855
Lennard, Barrett-	Horsford	2,124
Mack	Tunstead	2,168
Marsham	Stratton-Strawless	2,212
Montgomerie	Garboldisham	2,588
North	Rougham	2,580
Partridge	Hockham	2,741
Petre	Westwick	2,384
Postle	Smallburgh	2,185
Rolfe	Heacham	2,787
Stafford	Costessey	2,995
Thornhill	Riddlesworth	2,545
Unthank	Intwood	2,416
Villebois	Marham	2,370
Walker	Terrington	2,180

The following owned estates in Norfolk but no substantial Norfolk residence because their main landholdings were in other counties:

Ranelagh	3,043
Smijth	4,418
Buxton	2,152
Calthorpe	2,559
Rosebery	2,051
Spencer	2,533
Townley	2,866
Winterton	2,066

Source: Bateman, J., *Great Landowners of Great Britain and Ireland* (1883)

Bateman is the most reliable source on this subject. Nevertheless his list was not quite complete, for he omitted the Bacons, Blofelds and the Rogers and the Holmes of Gawdy Hall. For the purposes of research I kept to Bateman's list.

Index